In Writing

In Writing

Conversations on Inspiration, Perspiration and Creative Desperation

HATTIE CRISELL

GRANTA

Granta Publications, 12 Addison Avenue, London W11 4QR
First published in Great Britain by Granta Books, 2024

This book draws on interviews, some of which were aired
on the podcast *In Writing with Hattie Crisell*.

A CIP catalogue record for this book is available from the British Library.
1 3 5 7 9 10 8 6 4 2

ISBN 978 1 80351 063 7 (hardback)
ISBN 978 1 80351 064 4 (ebook)

Typeset in Bulmer MT Std by Iram Allam
Printed and bound by CPI Group (UK) Ltd, Croydon, CR0 4YY

www.granta.com

For Mum and Dad, with all my love.

Contents

Introduction

In March 2023, I took a train to Oxford, walked along the damp canal towpath and knocked on the door of the novelist Barbara Trapido, whom I was to interview for my podcast, *In Writing*. She made coffee, and we sat at the kitchen table with the paraphernalia of family around us. As rain fell on the roof, she told me the story of her life as a novelist – and in the course of the conversation, made an offhand remark that stuck with me. 'I think all writers are part of the same trade union,' she said, 'and we should support each other.'

Writing involves a lot of time inside your own head. As a journalist, I have on occasion been forced to write copy while surrounded by people – but even when I'm facing those deadlines in a noisy office or on a train, the act itself remains internal and solitary. It has many delicious moments, but doing it seriously is tough, and you can easily get lost and demoralised in that private space, trying to work out why the words won't cooperate. The more years I've dedicated to it, the more curious I've become about what it's like for other writers. The desire to open their kitchens, studies or sheds as though they were dolls' houses, and peer in at them as they frown at their notebooks and screens – the desire to see what common ground we all share, and what the essence of a writer might be – was at the heart of the podcast I started in 2019. Now it's at the heart of this book.

If you love to read and listen to good writing, I hope you'll enjoy this glimpse of the lives of some remarkable creatives. If you're grappling with this kind of work yourself, then you'll also find practical advice in these pages – but you'll have to choose what suits you best, as some of my interviewees contradict each other, making compelling arguments for different approaches. My intention therefore is not to tell you how to write, but to tell you how good writing happens to be done by some of the very best. I can promise you absolute solidarity: everyone engaged in this work is struggling with roughly the same concerns, which I've grouped into ten questions. They are my attempt to explore what it feels like to write, and to make writing your life.

They will shed light on what the writer's mind is doing while they stare at the page, and what compels them to return to it again and again. A lot of the craft of fiction, poetry, journalism and screenwriting becomes instinctive over time, with the eye, ear, hand and heart working together; as with driving, the more experience you have, the harder it is to describe. It's not easy, then, to find detailed explanations of the work itself, and so I have tried to be forensic in this book. I've looked more consciously at my own practice as a writer, and I've pushed others to articulate what they mean when they talk about having an idea or about honing the structure of a story.

Sometimes they had to be coaxed. The novelist Maggie O'Farrell told me that she's superstitious: she worries that if she looks too closely at her practice, she'll lose the knack. 'Are you going to make me talk about it?' she said. I confirmed that I was and, with a sigh, she gave in. I don't regret a single question. Her answers are fascinating and, to my knowledge, our conversation hasn't given her writer's block.

Fifty-five of my interviewees are quoted in this book. They vary wildly in what they do, from political commentary to TV drama, but I think I now have a sense of some of the qualities they share. Writing can be a very slow process, so it's tempting to say that you need patience – but I think what's actually required is determination that you will not be beaten by any problem that can be solved. You also need to be thrilled enough by both the subject matter and the feel of your project that you can't leave it alone. This is why the best idea is always the one you are excited about – not the one your friends and family like.

Perfectionism is part of it, but must be restrained until the right moment. Writers have to be forgiving, encouraging and indulgent at the start – to treat themselves as they would a child – because that's the best way to get words down, and a mediocre first draft is infinitely better than no first draft at all. Later in the process they become strict and exacting, as they transform a potato print into the *Mona Lisa*.

To be a writer you need life experience and plenty to observe, which everyone has, and the curiosity to reflect on it, which is more unusual; it's in this act of pondering that surprising connections can be made and ideas can flourish (a reward for the 'overthinkers'). As I write this book, creative work has started to be done by artificial intelligence. In a world where one day computer programs might write very well, what does it mean to express yourself as a flawed, emotionally weathered human being? It is our life experience that stands us apart from the most sophisticated technology. Computers do what they're told, and they do it perfectly, but humans sustain damage every day and come to things by clumsy, circuitous routes. We experience sorrow, humour, euphoria, frustration, humiliation, pride and affection: all of it makes our writing more meaningful and pierces it with points of connection for readers.

The conversations I've had with writers for this project have been frank, memorable and intimate. From Barbara Trapido at her kitchen table with her granddaughter's paints nearby, to essayist David Sedaris in New York, tidying his apartment as he made me laugh across the Atlantic, each of them has taught me something, and not just about putting words on paper. This book is also about what it means to write and to understand the world through writing. It is about one way that we can live: a way to examine and make sense; to connect, express joy and survive suffering. It is my trade-union invitation to you as a reader, and my love letter to writers everywhere.

Contributors

This book is gratefully drawn from conversations with the following people. Without them there would be no book, for more reasons than one.

JAMES ACASTER, stand-up comic and author, speaking on 8 March 2021 from his home in London

ANDRÉ ACIMAN, novelist, memoirist and essayist, speaking on 27 November 2019 while visiting London

AYỌ̀BÁMI ADÉBÁYỌ̀, novelist, speaking on 9 November 2022 from her home in Lagos

RUMAAN ALAM, novelist, speaking on 1 October 2021 from his home in Brooklyn

AMER ANWAR, crime writer, speaking on 25 September 2021 at his home in London

JESSE ARMSTRONG, screenwriter, speaking on 30 November 2023 at his office in London

MONA ARSHI, poet, novelist and essayist, speaking on 20 February 2024 from her home in London

ANDREW BILLEN, journalist and interviewer, speaking on 6 November 2019 at his home in Oxford

HOLLY BOURNE, novelist, speaking on 13 September 2019 at her house in London

CHARLIE BROOKER, screenwriter, speaking on 2 December 2019 and 10 December 2023 from his home in London

WENDY COPE, poet, speaking on 21 June 2019 at her home in Ely

CRESSIDA COWELL, children's writer and illustrator, speaking on 18 January 2021 from her writing shed at home in London

JOHN CRACE, political columnist, speaking on 2 September 2021 at his home in London

ELIZABETH DAY, novelist, journalist and non-fiction writer, speaking on 26 July 2019 at her flat in London

GRACE DENT, restaurant critic, YA writer and memoirist, speaking on 13 November 2020 from her home in London

KIT DE WAAL, novelist and short-story writer, speaking on 8 July 2020 from her home in Royal Leamington Spa

GEOFF DYER, non-fiction writer and novelist, speaking on 18 January 2023 from his home in California

WENDY ERSKINE, short-story writer, speaking on 3 December 2020 from her home in Belfast

TOR FREEMAN, comic-book writer and illustrator, speaking on 6 October 2022 at her flat in London

WILL HARRIS, poet and essayist, speaking on 12 June 2020 from his home in London

ANNA HOPE, novelist, speaking on 3 December 2019 in her writing cabin at home in East Sussex

JOHN LANCHESTER, novelist and non-fiction writer, speaking on 24 November 2020 from his writing shed at home in London

SOPHIE MACKINTOSH, novelist, speaking on 8 December 2022 at her home in London

EMILY ST. JOHN MANDEL, novelist and screenwriter, speaking on 24 October 2023 from her home in New York

MEG MASON, novelist, speaking on 18 August 2021 from her writing shed at home in Sydney

MHAIRI McFARLANE, novelist, speaking on 3 June 2020 from her home in Nottingham

LIANE MORIARTY, novelist, speaking on 8 September 2021 from her home in Sydney

DAVID NICHOLLS, novelist and screenwriter, speaking on 13 November 2019 at his office in London

MARY NORRIS, non-fiction writer and former copy editor for the *New Yorker*, speaking on 20 November 2023 from her home in New York

GRAHAM NORTON, novelist, speaking on 20 April 2021 from his home in London

MAGGIE O'FARRELL, novelist, speaking on 3 March 2021 and 7 December 2023 from her home in Edinburgh

RUBEN ÖSTLUND, film-maker, speaking on 2 December 2022 while visiting London

ROBERT POPPER, screenwriter, speaking on 29 June 2020 from his home in London

LUCY PREBBLE, playwright and screenwriter, speaking on 15 January 2021 from her sister's house

GEORGIA PRITCHETT, screenwriter, speaking on 3 November 2021 from her home in London

KILEY REID, novelist, speaking on 24 February 2020 while visiting London and by email in October 2023

JOHN RENTOUL, journalist, speaking on 16 November 2023 at Parliamentary offices in London

HUGO RIFKIND, newspaper columnist, speaking on 11 March 2020 at his house in London

JON RONSON, storyteller and author, speaking on 8 June 2020 from his home in the Hudson Valley

MICHAEL ROSEN, poet and author, speaking on 3 February 2023 at his office in London

SATHNAM SANGHERA, journalist, novelist and non-fiction writer, speaking on 2 August 2019 at his flat in London

GEORGE SAUNDERS, short-story writer, speaking on 14 December 2020 from his house near Oneonta, New York, and 30 November 2023 from Santa Cruz, California

DAVID SEDARIS, essayist and performer, speaking on 1 December 2023 from his home in New York

ELIF SHAFAK, novelist, speaking on 3 August 2021 from her home in London

ALEXANDRA SHULMAN, journalist and former *Vogue* editor, speaking on 18 May 2020 from her home in London

CURTIS SITTENFELD, novelist, speaking on 1 May 2020 from her home in Minneapolis

RAVEN SMITH, columnist and essayist, speaking on 24 February 2023 at his office in London

WILL STORR, long-form journalist and author, speaking on 5 November 2020 from a writing trip

BRANDON TAYLOR, novelist, speaking on 26 November 2020 from his home in Iowa

CRAIG TAYLOR, non-fiction writer, playwright and editor, speaking on 6 May 2021 from his writing shack at home on Protection Island, British Columbia

BARBARA TRAPIDO, novelist, speaking on 31 March 2023 at her house in Oxford

EMMA JANE UNSWORTH, novelist, non-fiction writer and screenwriter, speaking on 20 November 2019 at her flat in Brighton

ROBERT WEBB, novelist, memoirist and comedy writer, speaking on 5 May 2020 from his home in London

ZOE WILLIAMS, journalist, speaking on 22 December 2022 at her house in London

MEG WOLITZER, novelist, speaking on 23 October 2023 from her home in New York

Note on the text

This book uses material from spoken conversations, which always involve ums, ahs and incomplete and meandering thoughts. In the spirit of good writing, and with the approval of my contributors, I've done lots of editing. Discussions originally recorded for the *In Writing* podcast have been polished and reorganised, and I've had new, off-air conversations that live exclusively in this book.

1

How do we find flow?

'The things that writing depends on are
so complicated, and almost inarticulable.'

GEORGE SAUNDERS, short-story writer

What's the point in asking writers about the conditions
they prefer for work – the locations, hours and materials?
Everyone is so different. Some are comforted by background
noise and others can't bear it; one author crosses time zones to
find somewhere he can concentrate, while another feels that even
getting out of bed could kill her creative momentum. There are
those who do nothing for months and then write in increasing
bursts, their deadlines like finish lines towards which they accel-
erate – and there are others who tap away year round, diligent
and consistent, happy or unhappy, but always clocking off before
dinner. If you are looking for a definitive answer on where to sit,
how to arrange your desk and how much time to spend there,
good luck to you.

Still, we're captivated by artistic practice, and we want to know
the circumstances under which an imagination takes flight. I think
the appeal of these routines and rituals is that there's solidarity
in them. Writing asks for endless graft, and because all writers
happen to be human, we face the same two mundane challenges:

our resolve comes and goes, and our attention is fickle. Good work is really only possible with deep concentration and sustained effort – and a person's idiosyncratic need to edit on paper, or to keep an admired book in view as a talisman, or to go out for fresh air in the middle of the day, is really just a way of managing human weakness, so that the writing can move ahead.

Our habits evolve to suit us in the same way that slippers mould to the shape of our feet: incidentally and through use. This tends to happen in private, so that casual friends of James Joyce may not have known that he wore a white coat to write, hoping that the reflected light would compensate for his failing eyesight. Even the writer isn't always conscious of their quirks. I didn't think much about my requirements until I had to write this chapter, and some of what I found surprised me. Maybe when I've asked other authors over the years to describe their routines, they've been struck by the same strange sensation – freshly aware that it might be weird to keep a writing room dark all day, or to get up at 4 a.m. in order to act out characters' dialogue unheard.

One thing I did know, because people have been pointing it out for forty years, is that I'm not tidy by nature. As I sit now in the dim quiet of an October morning, there are books and papers piled on the surfaces behind me, in front of me beyond the computer and also on the floor to my right. There are printouts of drafts of this book scattered around my flat, bleeding red ink, and more of them filling the recycling box by the front door. Attention is a finite resource, and so I prioritise: if I think too much about tidying, I'm afraid I won't get the writing done.

You might assume that since I'm messy, I must be disorganised too – but in contrast my process is somewhere between methodical and neurotic. For this book alone, I kept to-do lists, schedules, spreadsheets and colour-coded digital folders, all regularly updated. Disappointingly, it dawns on me that they all kept track of more or less the same information: what I'd done and what I still needed to do, recorded again and again in different formats and to various degrees of detail. Nevertheless, this is how I have to work. I need to feel that even when the book resists order, it will not overpower me. Without this admin, I would lose my sense of control, and all confidence that I can finish anything.

I live and work alone, and if I now withdraw to a bird's-eye view, I see that my home is a zone of concentration. The noise of a London suburb has become silence to me: planes, two train tracks and a dual carriageway nearby; toddlers staging protests on the pavement outside; hedges being cut and lawns mown; endless building works. The only thing that punctures my attention is my neighbour practising show tunes at the piano, which makes me homicidal.

I've heard myself say that one of the advantages of my job as a freelance writer is that I can do it from anywhere – but that's a lie, I think. I repeat it to myself as an excuse to travel. When taken away to another city or country, with the simmering promise of novelty and fun, the part of my brain I rely on for writing becomes sluggish and uncooperative. I type for half an hour, perhaps lying on a hotel bed, then I put my cheek down on the duvet, or get up to investigate available snacks. Soon enough, I'm outside, and possibly holding a glass of wine. I need to live a life beyond my flat, otherwise I would have nothing to write down – but I also can't make serious progress unless I tune out the voice that tells me, 'You could be living *right now*.' The truth is that my best work has always been done at home alone, when everyone else is out of sight, mind and earshot. In the moment of writing, I have to focus inwards. Self-consciousness is a disaster.

As for deadlines, I do no work without them. Over the two decades of my adult life, ideas that might (I pretend) have been nurtured into bestsellers have instead idled and died in my brain – because in failing to develop them, I had nobody to disappoint but myself. Journalism suits me well, because there's always an editor who needs something urgently and a newspaper or magazine page that must be filled.

In learning about what other writers need to work, love comes up more than you'd think. Sometimes it's called by its name, but often it sits unmentioned in the room like a teddy bear on a shelf (many writers have given their childhood toys a retirement spot somewhere near their desk). 'I like to have gifts from friends around to remind me when the self-loathing and self-doubt hits – as it always does – that there are people who care,' says author and screenwriter Emma Jane Unsworth. Similarly, the novelist Ayòbámi Adébáyò has a token from her husband, the writer Emmanuel Iduma, hanging on her wall; it's a symbol of his faith in her ability.

When Lucy Prebble talks about the writers' room for *Succession* – a drama series so successful and glossy that you might expect its creative team to have operated as a ruthless machine – she describes it as 'probably the place I feel safest in the world'. Her words imply that ideas thrived there because they were fed by some form of love – or at least trust. 'You have to create that environment,' she says, 'and part of that is being kind and vulnerable.'

Even for more solitary forms of writing, another kind of company is often at play: the presence of work by other authors. My interviewees talked about the touchstones they keep close –

beloved books like chaperones, there to keep an eye on the standard of work being done in the room. To me though, 'touchstones' also suggests the relief of having something solid on which to place a palm when you've lost your way. Identifying the writers who mean something to you, and having them on standby, is an expression of love and respect for the job.

Some people can ignore all noise, all awkward circumstances and uncomfortable settings, and just get going, and we should all try to hone that ability – but in the meantime, most of us have developed workarounds. In this chapter, you'll find the worlds that authors have built to keep distraction at bay, and the tricks they use to hold and sustain both the motivation to write and the focus required to do it well.

If you want to write, you might try getting a study and filling it with comforts – or checking into a cramped hotel room, all hard corners and polyester blankets, and working until you've earned the right to leave. You could build an office shed, or go to the library, or make quick notes in the car. You could treat your space as a haven, everything in its right place, or let it degenerate, a week of coffee cups growing happy bacteria. You could aim for two sentences a day or twenty pages; start early or work late; light a fire or go for a run. Writers will use any method they can to make it easier – or even just possible – to string together 100 words, then 1,000, then 10,000, and have them mean anything valuable at all. It's whatever gets the job done.

James Acaster, stand-up comic and author

I used to have a really romantic relationship with writing. I used to love buying notebooks, and I'd sit down and write all the time. My life as an open mic stand-up, before I was making a living out of it, involved travelling constantly around the country, and I was always on trains with my notebook. I'd really make a big deal of the fact that I was writing. Sometimes I'd sit on a table for four people, and hope that other people would sit down and ask me what I was writing, so I could tell them I was a stand-up comedian, even though it wasn't officially my job. Really I worked in a kitchen.

That was OK until the second year that I did a show at the Edinburgh Festival, and it was very well-received. Because of that, I put a lot of pressure on myself for the following year's show, and it made me very stressed. I'd try to sit down and write every day, and it completely destroyed me. I lost confidence in myself as a writer and as a comic, and I produced a show that I didn't enjoy performing.

After that I never sat down and wrote stand-up again. I make bullet points in my phone; that's it. If it's good enough, I'll remember it.

John Lanchester, novelist and non-fiction writer

The room where I work is always a complete tip. I can't work in a tidy room. I have an unbelievable chaos of papers and gunge and notes: proofs of a *New Yorker* article from two years ago, a torn-off reporter's notebook, a copy of my last novel – it came out in Spanish not long ago, so I was doing talks about it. I've got a kid's soft toy rabbit, about six inches high, called Harvey, who I got in about 1966, I'd say. I've always had him somewhere to hand, so he's a mascot.

I've got a neolithic adze on my desk – a stone axe or chipping tool that's between 3,000 and 5,000 years old. I often hold it. It's a slightly totemic thing for me about tools, because the main things on my desk are pen and paper and computer. I like the idea of there being a connection with our deep historical past – the tools that we make the world with.

Are you somebody who prints out a lot in your writing process – is this why there's paper everywhere?

I am. If I'm working on drafts, I find it much easier to have printed text. I think I'm more likely to catch mistakes, more likely to see things clearly. I find it hard to chuck stuff away as well. I think untidiness helps me access my unconscious: somehow it's safer to let ideas come to me. I don't like mess, and the house itself isn't messy, but you know, I'm in the latter part of my fifties now and I've never not worked in a chaotic room – so it must be in some sense deliberate.

There's research around the idea of flow – that once you get in the place where you're working on something and it's moving along, that's actually quite a precious state and it's better not to interfere with it. If there are things that you know work for you, go with them, I think. If you're going to get three more paragraphs written if you ignore that smelly old cup of tea that's been sitting in the corner, then you're better off ignoring the smelly old cup of tea.

How much do you tend to write in one session?

Five hundred words a day when I'm writing fiction. I can write more than that – with journalism, I write 1,500 words a day if I've got a longer piece to do. But if I were to try to write a novel at that speed, I might have a week of work and then conk out and not have another idea for three months. The thing about the 500 words a day is that I'm often breaking off in mid-thought. I don't say, 'Oh, I'll just finish the paragraph.' It's 500, stop. Because that means the next day, you know exactly where you are. You sit at the desk and complete the thought that you had yesterday, and then you're off.

That's quite a cheering way to start.

I have found it so, I really have. The other thing is that 500 words a day isn't an especially challenging target, and when it's going well you can get that done quickly. When it's going less well, when it's sort of hand-to-hand combat – when you're having to slightly gouge it out – it's not too much. There are bits of books that resist you. Often, by the way, they're the things that readers really like – you know, it's not a sign of something being good or bad, you can't tell. But if it's pushing back at you and it's heavy going – well, you can do 500 words of that.

Also, it's not nothing. If you take off weekends and have four weeks' holiday a year and do your 500 words a day, you've written 250 days that year – that's 125,000 words. That's a fat novel every year for your whole life.

Brandon Taylor, novelist

I think comfortably I can write about 8,000 words a session; if I push myself, I can hit 10,000 words a session. I didn't realise that I wrote really fast until I started talking to other writers.

I wake up in the morning and I sit at my desk and write and write and write until my attention span runs out. Then I get on Twitter and waste a couple of hours there, and once I've wasted as much time as I feel OK wasting, I go back to work.

My friends ask me how I manage to tweet so much and write as much as I do. What I've learnt over the course of working on books is that being harsh with myself doesn't help my discipline. If all I can think about is how I shouldn't be thinking about wanting not to be writing, then I get upset; I get distracted by the fact that I'm distracted. So I try not to be too strict with myself. I let my attention wane. I try to give myself lots of patience and room to be distracted, and once the distraction ends, I feel relaxed enough to come back to work.

Kit de Waal, novelist and short-story writer

My home office is right at the back of my flat, which is a piece of a big Victorian mansion, and it's a beautiful room with lots of natural light. Every wall is exposed brick and it's got a parquet floor. It's got a sheepskin rug, two orange mid-century chairs and a lamp, and two huge doors that lead out, one to the house and one to the garden.

On the walls are three artists' impressions of quotes from books, and all of them inspire me to write the way that I do. The first is a quote from Jack London: 'I shall use my time.' Then there's one by Herman Melville: 'It's not down in any map – true places never are', which I adore. And the third is by Leo Tolstoy: 'All the beauty of life is made of light and shadow.' That's definitely something I try to incorporate into my work: the light and the shadow, and the humorous along with the terribly sad.

There are lots of books in here about the craft of writing. There are also a few novels that I like to have around because they are so well done, and sometimes I refer to them for tone or register or vocabulary. One of them is by Donal Ryan, who is a master at describing the ordinary. Another is Kevin Barry, because he's such a lyricist – there's a real musicality to his work. And Graham Greene, for brevity. I've got *The Heart of the Matter* over there with lots of tabs on the pages, because he could put a world into a paragraph, and somehow, you knew it. I don't know how they did these things, but it's what I aim for.

And how do you use that room? Do you have a routine?

I use the room both for general admin and for creative purposes – but I don't write every day. If I've got something to say, I'll do it, and if I haven't got anything to say, I won't. I don't beat myself up.

Meg Mason, novelist

I try to get to my desk by 8.30 a.m. every day and actually manage it about once a month. It wouldn't matter, except my tendency if I don't is to feel like the entire day is lost and I can't possibly salvage it. I'm trying to train myself out of it and believe what Hilary Mantel said, that 'all the world's a desk'. You carry the work around with you in your head, and of course some of the best ideas come when you're walking the dog. I'm also not a receptionist and I'm not a shop; nobody's queuing up for me to get here and open the doors – 9.47 a.m. is a perfectly good time to start writing.

And in any case, even twenty minutes of writing would be better than no writing, I guess.

Exactly. I think the only thing I've really learnt is not to have my phone remotely near me. I don't bring it out to my writing shed, because there's a level of thought that you can get to in twenty minutes, and then there's a level much deeper than that, which you need to reach in order to create good fiction. In between those two layers is a pain barrier that you've got to break through, and the only way to do that is just to sit there and wait for the discomfort to pass.

In that pain zone, though, is where you naturally reach for your phone, because it's a distraction and it's kind of analgesic, but actually it just keeps you coming back up to that top layer of thought. Then you have to repeat the process over and over, and it's the phone that's creating the pain in the first place. So I am quite stringent about that, leaving it turned off and in the house, or sometimes I'll put it in the glovebox of the car and make it an absolute hassle to get it. I heartily recommend that.

Could you describe the space where you work?

It's a little wooden shed in the garden of our house. Even though I had been a freelance writer for twenty years and always worked from home, I'd never managed to have a dedicated space for it. I think the worst place I worked was a hall cupboard. We took out every shelf except the middle one, which was waist height. I put a computer on it and then I would just sit in the hallway typing as though I was in an office, shielded by the doors on each side.

But novels are much harder to write anywhere, compared to short pieces for magazines. So when we were buying this house, my husband and I decided we would have the shed built – but as soon as we moved in, I was like, 'No, no, it's fine. We don't need to spend any money. I can just make it work.' And of course, you really can't. I wonder how many writers feel like they don't deserve a proper space, even though it is a job, not a hobby.

So now I'm here, and I sit and look onto the neighbours' beautiful jacaranda tree. Because I'm such a visually distractible person, I used to have my desk positioned so that I was staring at a white wall. But then I read that Nancy Mitford said – to paraphrase her – that anyone who could have their desk under a window and chooses not to is slightly sociopathic, so I moved it. It's better. She was right. It's much, much better.

Hugo Rifkind, newspaper columnist

The room I use as an office has a glorious view over to Alexandra Palace. When we moved here, I had my desk right in front of the window, and I spent my whole time looking out at the birds and the trees.

I did nothing. Now I have my back to the window.

Lucy Prebble, playwright and screenwriter

About three years ago I decided to rent a room twenty minutes' walk away from where I was living in south-east London. It was a very small space with just a desk and a chair, in a big old factory. I'd spent years not doing that, because I thought it was wasteful. It seemed really indulgent to spend money that maybe at some points I didn't have, when I had a flat that I could write from. Then one day I thought to myself, 'I really want to just try it, maybe for a few months.' That was a useful way of thinking about it, and it changed a lot.

I definitely did enough work to make the money back that I spent on renting it, which was only a few hundred pounds a month, because I got more done. It was incredibly useful in the fight against procrastination, because you go to a different space that isn't particularly fun to be in, where the whole thing is about writing. You know that when you've finished your work for the day, you then get to go home, which you get to associate with relaxation. That psychological divide was really helpful, and I wished I'd done it years before.

What about when you're part of a writers' room – how does that work?

Well, for a few months every year, a group of writers get together in a room, normally in south London, and we come up with the next season of *Succession*. That writers' room is probably the place I feel safest in the world. I think people are funny when they feel safe, or at least I am. I know the American writers' room cliché is of everyone trying to top each other, and maybe that does produce really good, funny work – of a different kind. But I would say that when you make a joke, forty per cent of the time it's bad, forty per cent of the time it's OK or good, and twenty per cent of the time it's absolutely killer. You have to be in a space where you feel you can make the forty per cent of bad jokes, in order for somebody to have the courage or comfort to make the twenty per cent that are going to absolutely floor you.

You have to create that environment, and part of that is being kind and vulnerable. When you're going in and seeing the same people every day for months, and talking about quite personal things, you get to know each other really well – sometimes when you're coming up with ideas, you're going, 'Well listen, when I broke up with so-and-so . . .' or 'When my mother was ill . . .'. You forge very close friendships. As a writer who has spent most of my career on my own with a laptop screen, I found it such a gift to have somewhere to go at a certain time, to be around people who were nice and made me laugh. It was like a dream. So I would say for me, it's the opposite of being competitive. It's a place where you're being paid to be vulnerable, and the best work always comes from that.

Maggie O'Farrell, novelist

I have a place right at the bottom of the garden. It's not very office-like. I call it my studio, and until about two years ago, it was a really quite dilapidated Victorian greenhouse. It was very beautiful but very spidery, and it blew down in a gale, so we kept its red-brick foundations and these brilliant architects rebuilt the glass for me.

Sitting in there is like being inside the ribcage of some kind of mythical creature, particularly late at night. It's very screened – on one side by a big stone wall and on the other side by thick conifer trees, so I'm quite enclosed, but at the same time completely open to the light and the elements. This time of year I have lots of thermals and very warm cardigans on, so I sit in there swathed in wool with my wood burner and most of the cats, and I'm completely isolated and very, very quiet. It has the world's biggest desk, and I spread out all my books and notes – pictures and postcards and photographs and maps and visual planning.

In the winter, before I can write, I have to clean out the grate, light the fire and coax it into being, which I find quite metaphorical. I have to kindle this flame and nurture it, and some days it catches really easily, and some days the wood seems damp and it takes ages – which is very like writing itself.

I don't have a routine at all. I think if you have young children and you write books, you have to roll with the punches, and the most important skill to learn is the ability to change horses in mid-stream. You can't be too precious about waiting for the muse to strike – you have to be able to do it wherever you are, at any point, on whatever surface you happen to have available. I've taken out a notebook and written in the car outside a house where my daughter's having a play date, or I've written while walking to school to pick up my kid. You have to be able to submerge yourself in that world very, very quickly, without too much faffing around.

Anna Hope, novelist

I drop my daughter off at nursery and then make a cup of coffee and start. I thought I would be less productive with a small child, but actually I think I became more productive. There's a sense that you don't have any other time: it's these four hours and that's it, and so I just go for it. I really enjoy that, actually – the extreme, quite brutal focus. Then inevitably, when I'm with my daughter, stuff will be working at the back of my mind, and so by the time I get back to the desk I'll have stored up quite a lot.

Do you make notes through the day to make sure you don't lose those thoughts?

I've done that a lot more since having my daughter. I also started using a Kindle when I was breastfeeding. When you're up in the middle of the night and you don't want to disturb other people, it's a great way to read. I would email a draft to myself and read it on my Kindle, and that was really helpful because it feels as though you're reading a finished book, and so the editing mind is, I think, slightly sharper. As I was reading I would make notes on my phone, and then I'd email myself the notes, and I'd have them when I came down to the cabin in the morning – so I guess the work wasn't confined to those four hours.

David Nicholls, novelist and screenwriter

I find it hard to write well if there are people moving around in the house. I find myself getting a little twitchy and irritated. Even a library is better than that, because there's an atmosphere of labour, so for a long time I worked at the British Library and the London Library. Now I go to my office.

There's a desk with a computer, and that's where I ought to sit, concentrating, in an ergonomic chair – but more often than not, after a couple of hours I find myself on the sofa, where we're sitting now, writing while lying down.

There are some things where you really need a desktop. If I'm working on a script, and a lot of that work involves moving things around, having previous drafts easily accessible, copying and pasting – it's more structural – then I really need to sit up straight and write on a desktop. If I'm writing fiction, then what I'm hoping for is a kind of flow, a loss of self-awareness, and without being pretentious, I want to be in a certain state of mind. I often find that I'm better off doing that while sitting in a comfortable chair or lying down. So I write between there, which is where I should be, and here, where I usually end up falling asleep.

Sometimes I find the silence at the beginning of the day a bit daunting, in the same way that a blank page can be, so I listen to quiet music in the hope that when the music stops, I won't notice. There are some pictures on the wall too. I'm trying to make a space that's personal. When I finished writing *One Day*, I thought the answer was to have a very harsh, uncomfortable space in which to write, so I hired an office that was just a desk and a chair. It was grim, like a prison cell, but it was deliberately chosen for its lack of distraction. That didn't really work out. Now I've realised that actually, family photos, postcards, music and books are good things to have around you as subliminal inspiration.

Geoff Dyer, non-fiction writer and novelist

Here in Los Angeles, I work in a loft, and it has the worst, most horrible kind of acoustic. It's all metal, glass and concrete, so it's very clangy. In London, I have a lovely book-lined study, and that really is an ideal place to work. As soon as you go into that room, the combination of the sight of the books and the acoustic they create is gently conducive to concentrating. Needless to say, this doesn't make writing any easier.

André Aciman, novelist, memoirist and essayist

Every few years, I get rid of 100 or 200 books – this simply not to have too many at home. If books come in, we have to get rid of others – because books can sometimes prove quite stultifying. You can feel suffocated by them.

Grace Dent, restaurant critic, YA writer and memoirist

I know that I shouldn't write in bed, because it's really bad for my back, and it's really bad for my mental health. However, this is very often where the actual grunt work of a book gets done.

At five o'clock in the morning, I'll be woken by that awful feeling that starts to follow you around when you've signed a book deal, had a bit of an advance, already spent it and not written any of the book. You wake up thinking, 'I really should have written at least 40,000 words by now.' I tend to get up and make a really strong cup of coffee and neck that, and then in the first chunk of the day, before everyone else is up and the emails start coming in, I will very often write a load of book.

It's not the most healthy way to do it. When I've finished, and I've ended up with really bad shoulders, I go, 'I'm never doing that again. I'm going to hire an office, I'm going to have somewhere I go every day.' The thing is, I've already got my own office in my house – but when I go in there, it feels too much like work.

Sometimes I feel an urge to start immediately when I'm in that early-morning panic, and even the thought of getting dressed feels like it might stop me from ever getting to the writing. I might get distracted along the way. Is that how you feel?

That's exactly how I feel. I don't want to spoil that unique energy, where my brain is empty but it's full of possibility. I just need to start, and if I have to go anywhere or do anything, I get really angry. That's why my house becomes so messy. I don't want to waste the energy on silly things. I don't want to spend from nine o'clock until half past eleven speaking to the council about why my wheelie bin has been stolen again – and can I have a new one? And can they deliver it on this day? And can I pay with this card? That will rob two and a half hours of my life, and at the end of it, I won't do anything. I am fully aware that I am a nightmare to live with – because when I'm in the book zone, months and months go by where important things don't happen.

With my memoir *Hungry*, I did write in other places, because it was the first book I'd written for ages, and yet again I was seduced by the idea that you go on retreats. People always say it to you: 'Oh, you should go away somewhere and write!' So I did – I went on a cruise ship, I went to some nice hotels. But I work really hard doing everything else – I present television, I present radio, I do all kinds of stupid things, and what I remembered then is that if I put in a chunk of time to go off by myself to write a book, I get there and I'm just on holiday. I love my own company. My literary agent and my TV agent are like, 'Grace has gone for ten days to Italy to write her novel, so nobody bother her,' and I'm thinking, 'Yeah, but really I'm drinking lovely cocktails and sleeping.' You leave me by myself and all I do is catch up on the sleep that I haven't had. I come back and I'm gorgeously refreshed.

I went on that crazy cruise. I got beauty treatments, and I went walking on the deck and I had drinks. I did get five or six thousand words done, but I should have done much more, because I only really worked a couple of days. I certainly needed that though, to go away and be somewhere else – because if you're seeing the same things every day, you're not getting your best work done anyway.

I'd written the first half of the book and then I couldn't do the rest, so I booked myself into a Premier Inn. My feeling with this was – and I've done it a couple of times – there's nothing to do in a Premier Inn. They're not bad hotels, but the only thing that you want to do is get out of the Premier Inn as soon as you can. All you have is a desk and a TV that's too small. There's no mini bar. If you want to eat, you have to go to the supermarket and buy really sad food, because you don't have a kitchen.

I really recommend that. These fancy writers' retreats where they say, 'Oh, we're going somewhere beautiful in Greece and we're going to walk on the beach every day and eat gorgeous food' – no. I say, book into a Premier Inn, where the only place that you can go is the Toby Carvery next door, and almost have a gun at your head to finish your book, and you'll do it.

Jon Ronson, storyteller and author

The room where I work is quite bare, because we spent all our money buying this place. It's got a chair, a desk, a running machine and a daybed – as a neighbour said to me, for the times I feel overwrought.

Out of my window, I can see the road, and there's a pond on the other side. The pond is beautiful, but unfortunately there are snapping turtles constantly trying to cross the road to lay eggs in our garden, and they get run over. So I'm spending half of my life leaping from my desk and running into the road to stop cars from hitting snapping turtles. Sometimes we have to wheelbarrow them to safety. It's a full-time job and it's been terribly stressful.

Do you lie down on the daybed when you get back?

Well, one time I failed to stop one from dying, and I basically lay down for the rest of the day.

Oh, I'm so sorry. That's upsetting.

I know, it is. But it's funny, because it's turtles. But it's not funny, because it's life or death.

Wendy Cope, poet

I find it slightly irritating when people talk about writing rituals. You want to be as flexible as possible and you want to make it as easy as possible for yourself to write. Some of my poems are written away from home. I travel around doing poetry readings and I've written quite a bit in hotel rooms – that can be quite fruitful. I still write all my poems longhand before they get typed out, so I don't need to take a laptop. I don't need anything. I can write on the back of an envelope.

These days, anything productive I do, I mostly do in the mornings. When I was younger, I'd get ideas late at night, and when I had a job it was a real pain because I didn't want to be kept awake by a poem if I had to get up. When I stopped having to get up in the morning it sort of stopped happening. These days I get tired. I go to bed earlier, wake up earlier. I'm old.

Charlie Brooker, screenwriter

My monitor and the keyboard are on a thing that you can raise up and down, so I sometimes write standing up. Weirdly, I find it a good anti-procrastination device, but it only works under certain circumstances, if you know what it is you've got to write. Say I've done the outline for a script and I know basically what the storyline is – then it's good to be standing up because I write more quickly, and I get less distracted. I don't think, 'Oh, I'll google how a submarine works so that this scene is more authentic,' and then two hours later find myself watching dogs catching tennis balls in their bums, or whatever. I don't do that, because it's a bit uncomfortable standing up, so I want to get it over and done with. However, if you're in the stage of trying to think up the storyline, or you're a bit stuck, it doesn't help at all.

The one thing I never thought I'd say is go running. People used to say to me, 'Oh, I love running, because I can think.' I'd think, 'You fucking liar. How can you think anything other than, "I wish this wasn't happening"?' But actually when you've done it for a while, they're right. I've had loads of ideas while running that I put straight in a script when I got home.

Will Storr, long-form journalist and author

At home, my study is a small room, and it has a blackout curtain constantly closed. It's got a light on the desk with a special sticker that makes the bulb glow as faintly as possible. It's basically a dark hole. I know that's weird. I think it's really about concentration, and an extreme minimalism.

I go away at least once a year, usually in November, to work. I like to go to Asia, and I don't adjust my sleeping – I keep to UK hours, so that means I'm working until about three in the morning, still feeling wide awake, and I get so much done. I think, 'Right, I've got nothing else to do. I've spent all this money to be here and I've got to make it good.'

I don't have kids – that's what enables me to do this – but even without kids, there are so many distractions at home: walking the dogs, answering doors, and people phoning . . . When I'm away, even when I'm walking around, I'm still in a bubble of thinking about the ideas. It's such a great thing to be able to do, because it's like an accelerator. I come back after two weeks feeling like I've done three months' work.

Barbara Trapido, novelist

I get up at about four o'clock in the morning. I discovered by accident that writing at this time of day is wonderful – partly because if you're quite a gregarious person, you can't start visiting cafes or phoning your friends.

I never write in a planned sort of way. I just muddle about, staring into the dark. It's much easier to get into that side of your brain at four o'clock in the morning, when you're still almost in a dream state. It's a real treat just to have the world to yourself and be interacting with a whole cast of pretend people.

I do a lot of talking out loud, which is another advantage of it being so early, because nobody's listening. If I'm writing a conversation, I do a lot of shouting into the mirror and crying, and I move the furniture and sit in different chairs. If people are around a dinner table, I need to know where they're sitting.

Mona Arshi, poet, novelist and essayist

I have my poetry brain and my prose brain, and the conditions I need for each are different. I think you really need to give prose your full attention and your central vision, whereas with poetry, you have to wing it. It's a kind of conjuring. Poems flourish in the inattentive space, around the periphery of your mind or imagination. They're very sly.

What conditions make it possible to write a poem?

I need a lot of quiet. I often start by reading my way in. I find that reading other poems that I admire, 'centre of gravity poems' if you like, reminds me what a poem is and what it can do.

I have a dictionary by my side and when I need something, a word might act like a trigger or almost a piece of kindling, and boom, there's something alive that I am curious about. It's funny, I was reading an interview with Ted Hughes, and he said he would often look at Sylvia Plath, and she would be hunched over her notebook, and there would be this massive dictionary at her side. I've spoken to other poets, and they do it too – it's as though the dictionary is your only friend.

Other times I might just work into a line that maybe I've written down, or a feeling or memory, and that line will operate as a sort of measure – in rhyme or in syllable count – and as a tuning fork. Of course, many other times there's the gulp-in-the-throat moment that you'll simply lean into. I use that feeling or word to ignite the poem. I don't know what to call it; I don't like to call it inspiration, but there is something reachable that I'm working into, worrying into . . . almost like prayer beads.

You said it's an inattentive space that you're in with poetry, but it doesn't sound inattentive to me – it sounds quite focused.

Yes, but I suppose you're not focusing on the poem that will come into being – you're intent on avoiding that, and on not imposing your will on something that might have a mind of its own.

Sophie Mackintosh, novelist

I make a playlist for each of my books. It means that if I'm wandering around doing other things, I can still be in the world of whatever I'm writing. While I was working on *The Water Cure*, I was commuting to and from a job every day on the other side of London. It was horrible, and I couldn't even read a book on the Tube half the time because it was so crowded. Listening to a playlist was a way for me to start thinking about plot points. Now, when I'm working from home, a playlist gets me in the mood to write – it almost acts like a switch. Wake up, have a cup of tea, listen to the song, visualise it, sit down and write.

Emma Jane Unsworth, novelist, non-fiction writer and screenwriter

My space is very sanctuary-like. I've tried to fill the windowsill above my desk with things I love. I like to have gifts from friends around to remind me, when the self-loathing and self-doubt hits – as it always does – that there are people who care, I'm surrounded by love and kindness, and there's a point to it all. I think every writer needs to feel that.

Liane Moriarty, novelist

A friend of mine gave me a beautiful hourglass – I think it goes for half an hour. I often use it if I'm stuck with my writing. The rule is that I just turn it over, and I have to write for that time. It doesn't matter what I write, and I'm not allowed to go back and edit. I'm not allowed to think about it too much, but often, if I'm stuck, that hourglass gets me going.

Ayòbámi Adébáyò, novelist

Opposite me when I sit down, there's a framed book cover that my husband gave to me. I think it was in December 2020. I was trying to finish *A Spell of Good Things*, which is my second novel, and I was having some difficulty, so he designed a cover for it and gave it to me as a gift. After that, I would often just look at it, and it helped me to keep going.

George Saunders, short-story writer

I wrote my first book at work, and so one of the things I've nurtured over the years is that if I see a forty-minute block, I can throw a little switch in my head and say, 'OK, sit down and work for that short interval.' I try never to discard a day. If the morning starts off in a crazy way and I don't get to my desk in time, when I was younger I'd say, 'Oh god, the world hates art.' Over the course of a life, though, if you can salvage a twenty-minute interval every week, that really adds up, so I try to be a little bit gentle with myself.

From teaching all these years, I've noticed that when a writer is above a certain level, a lot of it is what I've heard described as the talent for having talent. It has much to do with the way you allow or don't allow yourself to make progress – those obstacles you put in front of yourself, more neurotically than anything else. I tell my students that one of the skills we have to learn is to self-game a little bit. It morphs over into self-help or psychology. Each person has some extant level of self-obstruction, and writing is a place where we really get to see that and stare it right in the face.

You're at your house in upstate New York at the moment. Where do you write while you're there?

I'm working on stories in a porch on one side of the house. It overlooks some woods and there's a little snow on the ground, so it's pretty and super cosy. It's also connected to the kitchen, which I really like. When our kids were little and we lived in a small house, I loved that feeling of writing in the middle of the family activities. This is awakening a lot of those feelings. I can just walk over to the kitchen and have a little conversation and coffee, and then come back in and start again.

It's interesting that the things that writing depends on are so complicated, and almost inarticulable. Something about being in this environment has made a part of my brain come alive again. I once heard about a study that found that artists, in their artistic practices, emulate the habits of play they enacted when they were little kids – so if you were somebody who was given vast amounts of time to run freely, you might feel more comfortable working for hours. If you were someone whose parents used to check up on you periodically, you might actually self-interrupt. Somehow, being in a busy family setting works for me. The Catholic part of me that doesn't feel comfortable with doing well for very long gets a chance to say, 'OK, you did well for seven minutes. Now the cat just threw up, so go out there and earn another seven minutes of decent writing.'

Sathnam Sanghera, journalist, novelist and non-fiction writer

I need noise while I write, so I listen to hip-hop. I know no one else does this; people like silence or they listen to background music. But writing can be really boring, and I like to have occasional distractions. Maybe it's because I grew up in a very, very loud family. I'm at my best in the quietest room in a noisy house.

That makes sense. And do you prefer a particular time of day – are you someone who can write through the evening, or do you get your best work done first thing?

I tend to do most of my proper writing in the morning, when I have maximum concentration, and then I'll go to rewriting later in the day. When I'm approaching a proper deadline, I'm often waking up really early and working ninety hours a week. The way to get more hours out of my day, I've found, is to drink. I would have a gin and tonic at five o'clock and then I'd have a second wind. The writing wasn't necessarily of a good quality, but I definitely got more done.

Craig Taylor, non-fiction writer, playwright and editor

It's very quiet here in my writing shack on Protection Island, off the west coast of Canada – almost silent.

Do you find that it's a better environment for getting work done than where you lived previously, in New York and London?

Definitely. There's a sense of really capturing my morning here. I can get up early and be quite disciplined. Then by the time the afternoon comes, I can just relax and let the day fall apart from there.

I break down what I do every day in terms of how many pages I fill in a certain notebook and how long I dedicate to that. I'm a big fan of setting a timer for an hour and forcing myself to work for that time – I find the only way of having discipline is to go a bit over the top with it. You're working against the clock, and it's kind of fun, because you can break it down. You think, 'I've got five minutes to fill this page and five minutes to fill the next,' and so it's like a sprint, and it helps me turn off my mind and just move with my arm. For me, it's very gestural, and it's based on working quickly and not overthinking the sentences.

So you're writing longhand rather than typing?

Absolutely. I can't find another way to make it flow, to make sentences link up, to force myself to complete a line and go on to the next line. Like most people, I'm so damaged by smartphones that it's very tough to trick myself into thinking in a linear manner, and so this is a great way of doing that.

I think there's a forgiveness to writing by hand. Your handwriting is messy, the page is messy, the punctuation isn't correct – if you looked at that on a screen, which looks very much like a finished page, you'd feel demoralised. But this is more like sketching: you're making a drawing of your ideas of the day. It doesn't need to be perfect. That, for me, yields something much better than staring at a screen.

I've known you for a long time, and you are particularly good at being disciplined and protecting your writing time, your reading time and the things that you need to do in order to maintain the well-being that allows you to keep on writing and thinking. Where do you think that came from?

It's a fear of having life slip away, and more recently, reading about the attention economy and what we're up against. The particular stresses and challenges of our time include being faced with this technology that needs attention, and I'm just as bad as the next person in giving in to it. Ultimately, there's a sadness and a regret and a slight panic that creeps in, because if my attention, which is finite, is given to this, then it's not being given to that, and there's just so much to be done.

You have to consciously fight to safeguard your focus, because there are very strong and powerful and brilliant forces that can steal our time. I don't want to sound like a conspiracy theorist, but it almost is a conspiracy. I just want to look back and think, 'I read these books, and I did my own work every day. Whether or not it was published, it was mine, and it was in a notebook, so it wasn't something that Google or Twitter owns.'

I remind myself that this little shack where I work has to stay sacred – I have to get phones and computers out of it, because I'm lucky to have a space, and I want to keep it purposeful. I have a mantra too that I repeat to myself: *no crack in the shack*. I believe that these things are addictive, they are drugs, and so I say to myself, 'OK, there's no crack in the shack right now – you have to take your phone out, your computer out. You have to just be with yourself.' Maybe I'm crazy, but I'm walking around muttering that line.

Is daydreaming part of what you need to protect?

That's very important, but I can't really schedule it – so I believe in having a notebook at all times. My notebook is a partner that accompanies me through life and allows me to express myself in a different way. For instance, there's a little ferry that goes across the harbour – it takes ten minutes. That's a great place for daydreaming and letting my focus on the world soften to see what comes rushing in. But when ideas do come rushing in, man, it's great to have this little notebook – this little friend that is always nearby.

Mhairi McFarlane, novelist

I hate admitting this, because my editor is going to be like, 'I knew it' – but I am the deadline jockey. I really need the deadline to make me sweat, or else I will sit there playing around and trying to make it perfect. If you look at my word count, it's the stuff of comedy. A whole month goes by: McFarlane clocks up 5,000 words. Deadline week: 25,000 words in a day? Surely that's not humanly possible!

Wendy Erskine, short-story writer

I've never really had the idea of a room dedicated just to my work. I suppose my whole attitude has been that this writing needed to fit around what already existed. I was determined not to be precious about it in any way.

Normally I write in the kitchen. There's often a pile of dirty dishes. I don't need to have the place pristine before I make a start – I just zone out all of the mess. The same goes for noise; it really doesn't bother me if people come in and out and make themselves something to eat. I don't even mind having the radio on.

My kids have sometimes been quite critical of that. They've said, 'Once you're working on these stories, you don't hear a word anybody says. It's as if you've got imagination headphones on, and you don't even respond to us half the time when we're speaking to you.' I suppose that isn't very good, but it's just the way it is. I'm not constantly working, but it does happen that way at least a portion of the time.

Curtis Sittenfeld, novelist

I work most of the hours that my kids are at school. When I sit down, I write on a piece of paper what day it is, what time I'm starting and what page I'm starting from, whether it's page two or page 340. I think it helps me feel like I'm making progress, because it can be so incremental to write a book. It's also a weird ritual: I don't throw those pieces of paper away, even though they're essentially garbage. I might have ten pieces of paper that represent an entire novel at the end, and I feel sentimentally attached to them.

Is there a number of pages that you expect to have written by the end of one session?

It varies a lot, and I think that's part of the point of keeping that list – I'm saying to myself that this is an ongoing process and some days are more productive than others. Also, word count doesn't always reflect productivity. Sometimes I've only written 100 words, but I've had a really important insight into how to structure the book.

Every day I print out what I've written. It's kind of a back-up method, but also I had a writing professor who would say, 'When you start each day, look at the last sentence that you wrote yesterday and then continue.' Especially if you're writing a novel and you're on page eighty – don't start today by looking at page one. The easiest or most efficient way to finish a book is that you finish the book, you let it be really messy, and then you go back and fix it. You don't write one perfect sentence, and then move on and write another perfect sentence. I don't think I could finish a book that way.

So many things that help my writing are not about crafting sentences but about time management and organisation. Schedule it and treat it like it's an appointment with another person; look at your calendar and mark out, even for the next two weeks, when your writing time will be. Think through ahead of time what you're going to be writing and how you're going to start. What's the next scene? Or what are the first few sentences?

Clear off the desk beforehand, or at least think about where you will sit, and then when it is your writing time, sit in your writing place and don't do anything else. It's OK not to write, but don't get online, which is very hard obviously. Don't read a book, don't start cleaning, just sit there – and if because you're in this quiet mode, you think 'Oh my god, I should have answered such-and-such email three weeks ago,' which is the kind of thought I have, write it on a piece of paper next to you but don't do it.

It would be interesting to test this, but if one person read a book about time management, and one person read a book about writing tips, and then they both tried to write a novel – I almost think the time-management person would be better off.

2

Where do ideas come from?

'For me, it's not "write what you know",
but write what obsesses you.'

MEG WOLITZER, novelist

Welcome to the million-dollar question. As admiring readers or aspiring writers, we look at a wonderful novel, story collection or movie and we want to know about the imagination that produced it. Sometimes, its key idea is a witty conceit so simple that we feel we could have come up with it ourselves, but didn't (and after years of not coming up with them, you start to wonder if it really comes down to luck). Other times, the writer's vision is so wild that we can't begin to fathom how it came to them. We curse our own useless brains, which have never once murmured anything so arresting or lucrative as, 'Hattie, what if aliens landed, and a linguist was pressed into service in trying to communicate?'*

When you ask a successful novelist or screenwriter where they find their ideas, however, they often turn slightly scornful or even irritable. It can be an interview killer. They're dismissive of it as

---

* 'Story of Your Life' by Ted Chiang, which was later adapted into the film *Arrival*, nominated for eight Academy Awards.

a topic, and they don't know how to answer the question – or they've manufactured a slick and convenient response, because everybody keeps asking. The problem is that these answers make the process sound a lot more methodical than it feels.

After a number of awkward conversations along these lines, I've come to understand that it's a crunchy topic because it's based on a major misunderstanding about what an idea is. We've fetishised the thought that a genius will suddenly halt the conversation over dinner and scribble a sketch or a few words on a napkin. Eureka! It's as though with that, their work is practically done. Of course, it's true that the instant when the writer has their first thought for a project is important, or at least it seems that way when you look back. But is it really like a lightbulb illuminating everything? I think it's more like a flash in the dark twenty metres away.

In my experience, what feels more significant is the moment when you join the first idea – what you want to do – with the second, which is the way you'd do it (and in practice, as this chapter will show you, both of these can be fractured into several less conclusive moments). I'll give you an example. I knew in early 2021 that I'd like to write a book inspired by the interviews I'd been doing with writers. That was my Big Idea, I suppose, but of course it was a flimsy nothing. If you'd sat it down to talk, it would have intoned, 'A book inspired by conversations with writers,' over and over again, because it had nothing else to say.

Having had this idea, I tried to work out the best way to organise the book and present my material; I worked on it for months, moving it in different directions – a how-to, a memoir – and none of them felt right. Eventually, I parked it and went back to working on other things: my podcast, a novel, some journalism. I read unrelated stuff, I talked to friends and I watched TV. Idea schmidea.

Almost two years after I'd started, and with the project half-forgotten, I was making coffee one morning when the format of the book came to me quite clearly: ten questions that should and do preoccupy writers, with an essay on each, followed by an oral history of the process from some of the world's best. I could say that this more fleshed-out idea came suddenly – which it did in a way, if you discount the previous two years – but that makes it sound dramatic, which it wasn't. It felt unremarkable and obvious, as though I'd glanced to my left and noticed it lying on the kitchen counter.

I suppose this was a eureka of sorts – when I described it to screenwriter Charlie Brooker, he said, 'You got an email from your subconscious.' To get there had taken a lot of work and thought, however, followed by a long period of almost forgetting about it.

Once I started writing the book, it needed to eat a lot more ideas in order to live, and I was still supplying them right through the manuscript's editing process and almost until it reached the printer. I believe inspiration is not a lightbulb but hundreds of connected glimmers, like a net of fairy lights, and that they illuminate one by one as the work progresses. It's hard for authors to talk about this in interviews, because it's so workmanlike and long-winded – but it's true, and I think it's useful to know that from the start.

This is why you absolutely should not wait for a Big Idea before you begin. If what interests you initially feels insubstantial, that doesn't mean it won't eventually form part of the constellation of a very weighty project. Inspiration arrives little by little, and you can access it by chipping away, thinking, discussing, reading, writing, deleting, taking breaks and getting back to it.

It still feels like magic, and there is real exhilaration in the process, especially when your brain presents you with a connection it's been working on out of hours, without your supervision. In the end, it feels as though the project was there all along, and all you've done is uncover it. There will be moments when it will even feel effortless – but only if you forget all the effort you've put in.

Elif Shafak, novelist

It's like a pendulum. Writing is always at the centre of my life, but I'm an introvert by nature and when I'm working on a book, I become very disconnected. When the book is over, I become a relatively more social, normal human being. I like to go out and listen, and discover other disciplines, and just read and research until a story finds me. I don't rush it.

I honestly think writers need to be two things all their lives: we need to be good readers and we need to be good listeners. Both of those are about absorbing words and emotions, trying to understand this moment in time, and trying to hear what people tell us about their pains and their sorrows.

Jesse Armstrong, screenwriter

There's a whole hierarchy of ideas. There's an idea for a movie or a novel, and then there are ideas for tone and characters. There are ideas for structure within the novel or the episode, and then for structure within the scene. It's a long time since I've had a big idea for a new TV show, but I'm much more familiar with the feeling of, 'Suddenly I can see how we should restructure that episode' – and in a way, those are the more useful ideas, because they're the ones you have to deal with day by day. You can get through your career with only a couple of big ideas – maybe I'll write about politics, or maybe I'll write about the media – but you need a lot of the small-scale ones.

If you're at the beginning of your career, what might be worrying you is, 'What is my novel or TV show going to be?' I'd say try to take the pressure off. You probably already have the idea. You might be thinking, 'I want to write a relationship novel about people in their thirties, but probably everyone's trying to do that.' Well, no, that's your métier and I wouldn't overthink it. Sam Bain and I wrote the sitcom *Peep Show* about two men in their twenties while we were two men in our twenties. The material was there for us. You might think that you need to come up with something mind-blowing, and if that's how your imagination works, then great – but it might be that you're just going to do a really good version of the thing that seems almost too obvious to you to merit being an idea. It is an idea, because you know it inside out, and that's why you're going to be worthy of writing it.

And you're going to be able to flesh it out in a way that feels specific, and different to somebody else's novel about people in their thirties. One thing that was very innovative about Peep Show, *though, was the way it was filmed – from the characters' own perspectives, and with a voiceover of their thoughts. That was almost the big idea. Do you remember how that came to you?*

Yeah, and it's a good but potentially annoying piece of advice: collaborate and have lots of irons in the fire. That idea was just a solution to a problem. The original format was going to be two young men watching TV and making jokes over it, but we found that wouldn't sustain, so we wanted a conceit to turn into a show. We considered lots of different things, but Sam had watched a documentary called *Being Caprice* about the model Caprice Bourret. She wore a camera on her head and said what she was thinking as she walked around. We also thought about *Being John Malkovich*, and a few other famous works of art – there's a noir thriller, *Lady in the Lake*, and a bunch of other things that are shot that way, and we wanted to combine that with an internal monologue. I don't think we would have naturally come up with such an idea for a show had we not been looking for a solution to a problem.

I think aspiring writers can be so nervous about choosing the right thing that they can stall on diving in – but actually, it's once you're in the process that the ideas start coming.

Exactly. The roots of *Succession* were me writing a documentary that a producer had suggested, which was 'Business Secrets of Rupert Murdoch'. I couldn't do that, so I turned it into a TV play, but I couldn't get that made. Then ten years later, after I'd read a lot about other media moguls, it clicked for me: 'This could be a show about a fictional media family.' Writers often have the idea that they keep on coming back to, and I just kept on being interested in that world.

Are there conditions that you find particularly fertile for inspiration?

Other people. It can be collaboration with another writer, and for years that's been Sam. It's really about interaction with another brain, and that could be a dead brain in a book. I often get ideas from reading. If you're stuck for ideas, going for a walk is good, but better than that is probably to read the *New Yorker*, or the *New York Review of Books*, or anything that you like – that's the sort of stuff I like in that mode. I'm a magpie, and rather than necessarily reading a whole book about genetics or physics, I like the feeling of, 'Oh, I've read a review of this, and now I know a bit about genetics, and a bit about Renaissance Florence,' or whatever it is.

Having those different worlds in my head helps me get into the state where new ideas happen. You take something from one place and put it in another, and you start getting connections. For me, that's the feeling of inspiration: connecting two disparate things, perhaps a tone and a world. 'I've never seen that tone done in that world,' or 'I've never seen that relationship in a business or a family context.'

Kiley Reid, novelist

Especially with writing a novel, considering how long it takes to publish one, you have to believe in what you're writing. You shouldn't be writing what anyone else thinks is high art. You have to be obsessed with it. If you're not obsessed, then the truth of it will not come out.

George Saunders, short-story writer

I try not to have ideas for stories because I found out over the years that for me, An Idea is always capitalised, and the danger is that it's self-fulfilling. There's no surprise in it. It becomes a pedantic demonstration of what you intended. For me, the best form of inspiration is to try not to have too much at the beginning – just enough to get yourself interested, so that you start digging around in the dirt. Then day to day, inspiration is just the excitement that you might in fact have something going on, but you don't know what it is yet. That drives you to the room.

I really trust that feeling, because it produces stories that are free from my controlling, agenda-laced mind. It's almost the way a relationship works: if you have a big lofty idea about what a relationship is, it will probably keep disappointing you in the actuality. If you say, 'Well, let me see how this goes today,' and you have a couple of pleasant moments with the person and you're laughing together, then that feels more solid. I prefer that to an aspirational approach.

Most of the stories of mine that I really like started with a tiny notion that wasn't too ambitious, and grew by a series of surprises into something that had heft.

Could you describe what that tiny notion might be?

It can really be anything. The symptom that I've learnt to recognise is just a slight excitement: 'Oh, I can do something with that,' or 'That has legs.' In the case of the story *CivilWarLand in Bad Decline*, it was the idea of a shoddy Civil War theme park. It occurred to me, and the feeling was of intrigue, and almost of rubbing my hands together with glee – as opposed to the feeling of 'Oh, that's smart,' or 'That really will demonstrate some themes.' I've learnt to run away from that, because if you have that thought, then you've already written the story. If I feel like I can make some humour out of something, that gives me confidence, because I know that the meaning will follow. If I just try to make meaning, on the other hand, then nothing happens – no meaning, no nothing.

An idea tends to gestate for a little while in my back brain. I also keep a file of good bits that I've cut out of other stories. There might be a scene that I've worked hard at, that's really funny – but it's an energy-blocker in the story in which it's appearing, and doesn't need to be there. I'll pop it out and set it aside. I've had several of those in the last ten years: you send it to its room, make it stand in the corner, and it starts to go, 'Oh, yeah, that feels better. I didn't want to be in that story in the first place.' Then it starts to send out tendrils of its own. It wants to do all kinds of things that it couldn't have done in that original context. That's a kind of inspiration too: if you're patient with any bit of writing that's working, a story will start to form around it. You just need a fragment.

Do you tell anybody about your fledgling stories before you've finished writing them, or do you feel that you have to guard them until they're strong enough to share?

Sometimes I'm excited about it, and I tell my wife – but on the whole, my feeling is that it's best not to. If you release the pressure by talking about an idea, that's creative energy that you would have used in writing if you hadn't popped off about it to somebody. I also feel that talking about it locks it in place. If the person you're talking to says, 'Oh, I love this,' then you'll have a hard time changing it; if they think it sounds stupid, then you're going to lose faith. People work in different ways, and some writers really need that interaction, but in my experience, the longer I can keep it to myself, the better it's going to be.

Do you think we can get better at having ideas?

By trial and error, I think we improve our instincts about which ones to turn away from and which ones to embrace. I had a teacher once who said that if a young writer could tell the difference between a story he thinks he should write and the story he should actually write, he'd save himself about fifteen years. Again, it's a bit like relationships. After you've dated a bit, you know that, 'Yes, this is interesting to me – but it's going to turn out badly, so I'm not going to pursue it.'

Don't imagine that you need to have a big idea. Even if you can think one up, it's hard to make it live on the page. Some people get caught in endless loops of worrying, 'Oh, that's not a big enough idea for my novel. I'll wait' – so then they're not giving the idea a chance, because they're not writing it. Others get too attached and keep telling themselves, 'Well, this must be a good book, because it's a great idea,' even though the book is screaming, 'I'm not! I'm not good! Stop pinning me down. I have things I want to do, but you're not listening.' I think we can taint a story a little bit at the beginning with too much intention, and it's very difficult to write your way out of that.

People tend to think that imagination is somebody sitting down and thinking of *The Wizard of Oz*, or some crazy concept. That's a very inhibiting view of imagination, that it's about having an unfettered mind. What a story actually wants, and what a reader wants, is some kind of spontaneity, but the idea is just the context: the spontaneity comes through when you're present to it, and react. Often it comes from refining what you've written, and waiting, and refining, and waiting, until you kick open a little door to the subconscious and you know what to do. Is that inspiration? Kind of, but it's mostly hard work.

David Nicholls, novelist and non-fiction writer

The terrible truth is there's no real recipe and no process I can go through that I know will result in a novel. It's different every time, and having written the fourth novel doesn't make writing the fifth one any easier whatsoever. You might learn things line by line about technique, and editing, and first person, third person, present tense, past tense – but you don't get better at being inspired, and that is the hardest part.

I'm really fond and proud of all of my novels, but I know that some are better than others, and I know that the writing is not consistent, and perhaps the next one is going to be a disaster. That thought is always next to the other thought: 'How exciting! I can write anything I want.' There's nothing stopping me from sitting down this afternoon and putting pen to paper – no one's going to see it, no one's going to publish it against my will, I can do anything I want – but that in itself can be quite intimidating. The freedom of it is both exciting and stalling.

Charlie Brooker, screenwriter

Often for *Black Mirror*, I'll have a concept but I won't know what the story is, and I can't do anything with it until I do. I'll hold it at the back of my head until I find a place to use it, almost like having an earworm, and that can sometimes take years.

We did an episode in the sixth series called 'Joan Is Awful'. The title had been in my head for a long time, and it came from a thought: 'Wouldn't it be weird if a normal woman woke up one day and found she was on the front page of the *New York Times*, with a huge article about how people don't really like her, and petty interviews from her co-workers?' I thought it was a funny idea, but I didn't know what the story would be.

Later, I was watching *The Dropout*, which was a dramatisation of Elizabeth Holmes and the Theranos scandal. The events were all very recent, and I thought, 'Ha – next we'll see her go home and switch on the TV, and *The Dropout* will be on.' I was thinking how weird it must be if you're the person at the centre of these events, watching a dramatisation of your own life, and then I realised: that's what the 'Joan Is Awful' story should be.

It also congealed with another thing I'd been thinking about, which was wanting to do an episode about AI technology. It occurred to me that this would be how an ordinary person would get a TV dramatisation based on their life – it would be generated by a computer. That led me to another thought: what if it used deep-fake technology to have your part performed by a Hollywood star?

Suddenly, you've got a thing that feels almost more thought out than it is. It's as though the ideas were three individual raindrops going down a windowpane, and then they ran together.

My impression is that your ideas often come from taking an absurd hypothetical, and then following it to its furthest logical conclusion. You pursue it down the line to see what it would really be like and what its impact would be.

Yes, that's often it. I'm a real catastrophist in everyday life, and I'm constantly imagining extreme possibilities. If I see an ice puddle, I think, 'Oh my god, what if I slipped on that ... and caught my eye on a hook that was protruding from the wall . . . and then I had to pull my eyelid off?' My brain leaps across those doomy lily pads very quickly, and I can't help that, but it's quite useful for writers of comedy and also of horror. Certainly with *Black Mirror*, often we have one MacGuffin – a trigger in the plot – and it unfolds until everything spirals out of control. There's a logic to it: the first idea begets other ideas and describes everything else in the world, in a way.

It suits me and suits the way I write, but I'm always slightly mystified by and jealous of what other kinds of writers can do. My ideas tend to burn themselves out quite quickly: it's difficult to turn them into returning series. I don't know how to do TV dramas that rest on excellent character studies. I'd be going, 'But what if he turned into a helicopter?'

I'd like to do a returning series where I could get to know the characters and the actors over time – it would make the writing richer. For me though, the problem would be finding a central premise that wouldn't worry me as being too pedestrian. If you said to me, 'Your next show has to be set in a bakery,' that would terrify me. Ideas have to fight for your attention, and that one wouldn't seem shiny enough – but I would probably watch somebody else's compelling drama set in a bakery, and I'd be full of envy.

Elizabeth Day, novelist, journalist and non-fiction writer

I like to allow ideas to sneak up on me, and I'm a big believer in the right idea coming at the right time. You need to be patient and let it happen, and a lot of the time, if it isn't happening, it will be because I'm overworked. I need to allow myself some space to let thoughts percolate. It's partly why exercise is really important to me, because I spend so much time in my head that I need to physically get back into my body. I find that's a very fertile time for thoughts to come – when I'm not actively making a decision to think.

Brandon Taylor, novelist

For your debut novel Real Life, *you drew on your own experiences. How does that affect how you approach a second novel? Are writers always drawing on their own experience, even if it's not as direct as that?*

I didn't write for a long time after I finished *Real Life*, because I felt like I'd used up all the material in my life – but what I found was that my writing got better when it became interested in more people. It got more interesting to me as a writer, and so I feel like I'm still telling stories that are important to me, but for different reasons.

The thing that drives me is this desire to tell stories about and for queer black people. I want to put people who resemble the people I love most in the world – my friends – into stories. If I'm not drawing on my experience, then I'm drawing on my observations about the world and I'm still telling stories that are deeply personal and important to me; it's just that the one-to-one correspondences are less legible. I've written several books that are yet to be published, and there are parts of myself in all of the characters, but the reader won't be able to say, 'Oh, this is Brandon's fascination with this or that' – it's hidden. Part of that is me maturing as a writer and just getting better; part of it is that I've told the direct story, and so now I have to tell the oblique ones.

Holly Bourne, novelist

Living makes you the best writer, and I try to live and learn as much as I write. I'm in training to be a counsellor and I love it; I'm learning about humans and relationships and attachment theory, and it's fascinating, and it obviously informs my work. I try to go to the theatre a lot too, and go out and converse. It's usually when I'm having the same conversation repeatedly with different friends that I realise, 'Oh, there's something in here.' That's the zeitgeist of the human experience at that moment in time.

Meg Wolitzer, novelist

In my case, an idea tends to be like a stone I throw, and then I paddle after it – and that's the writing of the book. For me, it's not 'write what you know', but write what obsesses you. There will be things that have been bothering or preoccupying me, and that's not quite the same as inspiration – but why not write about what you're thinking about anyway? Otherwise, it's as if writing is this separate thing that isn't connected to who you are, and what your passions are, and what you observe, and I think they're really inextricable. You're marinating in the world, and your concerns can have such a fervent quality if turned into fiction. So I'll take something that I realise I've been thinking about, and I'll start thinking about it more directly – and it's as if figures arise from hot lava and become representatives of how to talk about it.

With my novel *The Wife*, I was interested in male power and female complicity; I knew right away that the story was going to be in first person and that the character who would tell it was an angry, funny, pissed-off, older woman. The inspiration was just being in the world for as long as I had, so it was easy and almost a relief to transfer some of that to characters and make it into fiction. What interests me is how do people live? And what is it like? That's my mantra again and again: what is it like?

Have you had ideas in the past where you've spent time working on them, and then ultimately concluded, 'No, this doesn't have legs'?

Oh, yeah. I sold a book based on Freud's Dora a long time ago, and I travelled to Vienna to work on it – but I felt constrained, almost corseted, writing that story. I broke out of it and wrote *The Wife*, and I felt free. Real excitement needs to be part of writing. This is not homework. Writing can't be exciting all the way through, of course, but to me it's great at the beginning not to know what a book is. With *The Wife*, or with any of my books, I had no idea where it was going to go, but I followed it. I think that if you can't find that sense of play and freedom at the beginning, I would question the enterprise.

Then as you progress, it's a question of trying to remember why you were excited to begin with – it's sort of like falling in love. What was it that sparked you? Can you remember that?

Mona Arshi, poet, novelist and essayist

So much of what poets are concerned about is to do with the incidental and peripheral, which we can accidentally stumble on, so I don't have an agenda of what I want to write about. The ideas are often surprises. I do keep a notebook; I suppose you could call it my 'I don't know' notebook. I don't know what's going to happen to the stuff I write in it, but it's interesting to me: maybe it's a phrase I heard a mother use to a child on the bus, or a line I've heard on the radio, or a memory that popped up that I might poke around in.

Often a poetry collection has a theme, but I think that poets only understand what that is after we've maybe written twenty poems. You look at the work, and your poems have started almost talking to each other in juxtaposition. The last collection I wrote was really about women's silence – but if I'd known that at the beginning of writing it, I don't think the poems would have worked. Poems that are steered by an agenda I think invariably go wrong. What a good poet should do is try to get out of the way of the poem, and not press too hard on what you think you want it to be. Your role is shepherding, not imposing yourself.

It almost sounds spiritual, but I don't mean it to sound spiritual, because obviously, there's skill involved at the editing stage, which comes afterwards. That's really important. I've judged a lot of competitions now and I can see that so many people just stop after the first stage. The part that makes the poem work is all the other work that comes next: thinking about form, lineating it so it's active and on its toes, understanding syntax and trying to put yourself in the reader's position. That is the hardest part of being a poet – divorcing yourself from what you've written and trying to put the editor's hat on.

Wendy Erskine, short-story writer

When I first have a bit of an idea for a story, I don't do anything other than think about it for four weeks or so. I might be finishing off one story, but at the same time, I'm thinking about the next one – and I really just turn it over in my head, the various characters and possible eventualities. It's a really lovely part of the process, because everything at that stage is an abstraction. Nothing has been committed to paper anywhere at all. It's full of exciting possibilities. It's like you've got money in your pocket and you're going to town, and you're wondering, 'What am I going to buy?'

And so you're not keeping notes at this point?

No, because I'm a crappy note-taker. I'm shambolic with these things. I've had so many conversations – 'Has anybody seen the magazine that I stuck my important notes in? I think Neil Young's on the cover.' I'm constantly having to search the computer, and then when I find the file I realise that there's practically nothing in the document that is any use to me anyway. So I don't make any notes, I just think about it and hold it in my head.

Once that's together, I write a first draft with no restrictions at all. Sometimes I might shift the narrative point of view five or six times in it, or I might write stuff that I know there's no way I'm going to use in the end but it's just enjoyable. So that would be a normal way of working, Hattie, where I would maybe do a draft that's even 20,000 words for what will be a 6,000 word story.

Then I sit down and I try to read it in a really critical way. What's the focus of this? What am I really trying to deal with here? Quite often, something that I've thought is going to be central is really peripheral, or a character that I've thought would be an unimportant bit player becomes more interesting to me than somebody I thought of as a main character. Then I start again from scratch, working in a much more confined and refined way.

Barbara Trapido, novelist

I've occasionally borrowed people from life, but it doesn't really work. I find that characters borrowed from real life stay two-dimensional, where the ones that come out of the back of your brain do not. Maybe they're all versions of yourself.

Ruben Östlund, film-maker

For me, it's very important to have the whole film physically in my body before I sit down and start to write it. I talk about the project a lot. Before I write, I know how to pitch the project from beginning to end, and I learn so much from telling other people about it.

I use the people that I'm pitching to as an instrument. It tells me, 'Oh, now they're not 100 per cent concentrating. Here, they didn't react in the way that I wanted them to react.' I adjust parts of how I'm telling it, or I might swap the positions of two scenes.

That reminds me of the way stand-up comedians work, in that there's a constant processing of audience feedback. Did the audience laugh more when I used this word or the other one?

There's that awareness of the response all the time.

It's interesting that you mention that because I went to Los Angeles with one of my co-producers, and one of his friends is the comedian Larry David. I was sitting around a dinner table with a couple of comedians and Larry, and all of them had small notebooks in their inner pocket that they took out after they had tried some material. It's very similar. If someone had a comment on what they were doing, then they would write that down, and I'm doing the same thing – I'm trying to remember great notes that people have given me while I'm performing this pitch for them.

The idea for my film *Force Majeure* changed a lot because of this process. I was going to make a film called *Tourist*, following three or four different stories set in a tourist environment. I was about to start writing it when I told a friend about the scene with the avalanche: I said, 'A family is sitting at an outdoor restaurant when, all of a sudden, an avalanche comes running down the mountain – and all of them flee in panic. Then it turns out that there's no catastrophe, and they come back and they are ashamed.'

My friend went away and thought about it. The next day, he said, 'What if it's only the father who runs away?' When he said that, I thought, 'There's the idea.'

Hugo Rifkind, newspaper columnist

At the moment, you write three columns a week for The Times. *I know journalists who've had columns and have found it nightmarish – the pressure to keep coming up with something new every week. How do you approach it?*

In a tumbling panic kind of way. The op-ed column is particularly hard because I write it on a Monday; theoretically, you can come up with an idea over the weekend, but the news just doesn't work like that. The news starts each week on a Monday, so generally I wake up in the morning with nothing. I spend some time wandering around downstairs, growling, ignoring my children and snapping at my wife, listening to the radio and just trying to get something to spark. By nine o'clock, I've somehow communicated what I'm writing about to the comment desk at the paper.

It is a nightmarish process, but I've been writing some sort of opinion column now for maybe sixteen years, at least once a week, and I've always had an idea in the end. Although it's a ridiculously stressful process to go through, I've never not come up with the goods in time. So even while you're pacing around trying to figure out what the fuck to do, on another level, you're intensely relaxed in the belief that it's going to be fine.

Tor Freeman, comic-book writer and illustrator

I really admire how creatively curious you are, and how you dip in and out of different disciplines. You took an improvisational comedy course, and you sew and make your own clothes, and you do life drawing, and you read a huge amount, and you watch a lot. I wonder whether that very textured selection of inspirations leads to more original storytelling.

Well, most of my stories are about the things that have gone in – the books that I've read, often when I was young, or the films I've seen. Those are the things I'm interested in referencing when I'm telling a story. The starting point is that I'm trying to talk about something I've really enjoyed.

At the beginning of my career, I was always worrying about

how to write a story that someone hadn't already written. I think that's what we all think about when we start out, but over the last five or so years, I've let that worry go. I'm not going to try to write an original story, ever, and I don't think that would be my strength. I think it's about interpreting, through the characters that I can make, a story that's probably been written a million times. The texture you're talking about is everything that goes into you, everything you've read – and if your particular love is Regency romances, then that's going to come out in your work.

Emily St. John Mandel, novelist and screenwriter

As you get more experienced and more confident as an author, you start to feel like it doesn't even matter whether the initial idea is cool. I can write a novel based on it and make the novel good, regardless. It's just a starting point, and I'm going to build a world around it.

That's such a reassuring thing to be able to tell writers who are starting out, because there can be a real paralysis that comes with feeling like your idea isn't strong enough.

You know, somebody sent me a really excellent novel recently about the Second World War, and my initial response was, 'Oh god, another one – how many dozens of these have I read?' But it did feel original and special. It is the most mined subject, and there's nothing remotely new or interesting about writing a novel about it at this point – and yet people still write novels about the war that feel fresh and breathtaking. That is all down to execution. The idea just has to start a process that ends with a book that isn't like anybody else's book.

How do you think you get to that?

I think you have to be a little bit brave. You have to take the risk of looking ridiculous, which is easier for some authors than others, and maybe easier with time – or it has been for me anyway. My most recent novel, *Sea of Tranquility*, is about a time-travelling detective – there's no way I would have written that ten years ago. It would have seemed like career suicide, because I consider myself a literary novelist and yet here we are in the moon colonies. I think you have to be willing to follow the weird idea wherever it leads, and if it's too weird you can pull it back, but I think that's the only way to write something that feels original.

David Sedaris, essayist and performer

Maybe it's a personality thing, but because of the nature of my work, I exploit everyone and everything I come into contact with. Everything is possible material. I carry a notebook and I'm constantly on the hunt for something that will be strange or funny or tragic. I'm eager for it.

I guess I'm at peace with the fact that I use people. If I really sit down and examine it, I should probably be ashamed of myself – but I don't think I'm any different than any writer who's ever lived. Even if you're writing fiction, you're still looking at the world for material. One time I went into a hotel room and pulled back the curtains, and there was half a sandwich behind them. Even if I were writing a fictional character, if that happened to me, I would put it in.

I always keep a diary, and I'll give you some examples of things I've written down recently:

Last week, the language app Duolingo taught me to say, 'Why

are you going to the beach with your doctor?' in German. I thought that was so good.

I was at the airport just before Thanksgiving, and it was a horrible time to be flying, and there was a woman at the TSA Pre-Check who was not prepared at all. She turns around, confident in my accord, and says to me, 'You never know what they're going to ask you for.' And it's like, 'Yeah, actually, you do. You always know what they're going to ask you for.'

I met a man named Jaimer and a woman named Cader, and another man named Chayson. I wrote those down because these new names make my flesh crawl.

Another day, my boyfriend Hugh joined me at a hotel in Seattle, and we went downstairs to have breakfast. The host of the restaurant looked at me and said, 'What a lovely family you have.' I thought that was so great, because what he was really saying was that Hugh is good looking. So I looked down at my feet as if there were children down there, and I said, 'Did you hear that?'

Then one day I was in Arizona, and we drove past billboards picturing Israelis who were being held hostage by Hamas. I didn't expect to see that in Arizona, and that was interesting to me. I'd like to eventually write an essay about this time – so I'm collecting all kinds of stuff and putting it away for later.

Do you think that for a diary entry to inspire you to write an essay, you need a string of things that you can link together – so that, for example, the Duolingo thing could become an essay if you had other thoughts that linked to it thematically?

Yes. I put it in a file that I have on Duolingo, so I might be able to come back to it. Then there are also times that my life just feels like a story. I was at a restaurant in Australia and they had kookaburras on the lake, and a waiter said, 'Here, feed one.' It brought me back to a moment in my childhood, and it just unfolded: the whole essay was right in front of me. Usually I can feel it when that's happening, and I get nervous, because I don't want to get in the way of the story. I don't want to say anything that's going to end the conversation; I don't want to control it – but I want to urge it along.

Geoff Dyer, non-fiction writer and novelist

There's a wonderful bit in the introduction to the Thomas Pynchon collection *Slow Learner* where he refers to marijuana as 'that useful substance', and for many years it really was so useful to me, in terms of the uninhibited outpouring of ideas, and not being too clenched and uptight about editing myself as I went along. Even before that, quite often I'd be having an experience, and it was the fact that I was under the influence of some drug that made it seem worth writing about. In every way, it was positive, and I feel I was in a classic romantic tradition there – some of my experiences of drugs were like Wordsworth's 'spots of time', but in adult life, and I wanted to preserve them in print.

Then, at a certain point, it stopped working for me. I was living in London, and as people know, this great change occurred in the marijuana market. It stopped having any relation at all, it seemed, to the drug I used to like; it became this horrible thing that felt more like a traumatic head injury, and it was just too strong. You might think, 'OK, it's stronger, therefore I can use less to get the same effect,' and that would have been nice, because smoking was always so vile to me – but it seemed no, it wasn't just a thing of quantity. The whole nature of the experience was different. It wasn't one I enjoyed, and it didn't seem to be doing anything for me creatively. Marijuana stopped being useful at all, to my considerable surprise and disappointment, because I thought it would be something that would always work.

John Lanchester, novelist and non-fiction writer

People in the modern world think of everything in terms of careers, but in lots of respects writing is more like prospecting for gold. It's not really a career. You just go out and try to find something, and the fact that you found it once might be good luck or good judgement, but it doesn't mean you're going to find anything next time.

One of the challenges is to stay interested, stay open to new things, and try not to get stuck. I've always fed off doing journalism for that reason. I write a few pieces a year for the *London Review of Books* to keep my hand in and to keep thinking about new stuff, basically. You can get to a point, if your work's going well as a writer, where you end up not connecting with the world. That's slightly paradoxical, and there aren't too many careers that are quite like that: if you have a book that does well, it can allow you not to engage with people, not to go out, and not to listen.

I had the idea for my first novel back in the mid-1980s, when I was a graduate student. I thought it would be interesting to have a book that pretended to be a cookbook but was actually a novel, and I knew it had to be a murder story. Then having had that idea, I sat on it for about four years, thinking that one day I'd wake up in the morning and find that I'd written the book. 'Oh look, there's a manuscript by the bed!'

If only that were how it worked.

Yeah, I can exclusively reveal that that's not how it works. On some level I did think that having the idea was the main bit. It's a funny thing, because it's a question you're often asked: 'Where do you get your ideas from?' I find it hard to explain the extent to which the idea is not the main thing.

3

What's so hard about writing?

'How do people do this?
How can there be so many books in the British Library?
Why doesn't everyone just give up?'

RAVEN SMITH, columnist and essayist

Is there anything you find particularly difficult about writing?
This is the question I ask every writer I meet. When I asked Graham Norton, the comedian and chat-show host, who has in middle age carved out a successful second career as a novelist, he answered thoughtfully. 'Starting,' he said. 'Starting, and finishing, are the hardest bits.' He paused. 'Keeping going is also very difficult. Those three things, I think, are the hardest.'

The creative life is the only one I've ever wanted – but there's no getting around the fact that the work is awfully hard in all its phases. Even if what you're doing is academic or technical, it feels so personal. You choose the words, you build the sentences and you try to share ideas that make up the fabric of yourself – you tear flesh from your heart and you put it on a page. Then you send it out to be treated carelessly by strangers, because writing is only solitary work until it isn't.

I'm embarrassed to tell you that from time to time I have cried about my writing: shameful tears that came from the abyss between how good I wanted a piece to be and how very un-good it was. The most painful moments are always when I'm trying to stretch my skill to something new, because in the background lurks the suspicion that maybe this is it: potential already reached. I've been in the depths of self-loathing and despair, wondering what the hell I will hand in to the editor who is waiting for it, so I understand how the writer Dorothy Parker felt in 1945 when she sent a forlorn telegram to her own editor, Pascal Covici. 'This is instead of telephoning because I can't look you in the voice,' it said. 'I simply cannot get that thing done yet never have done such hard night and day work never have so wanted anything to be good and all I have is a pile of paper covered with wrong words.'

Most writers agree on the pain of it all – in fact, complaining about it is our disagreeable shared hobby. In our defence, nobody complains with more panache than us. In Franz Kafka's diaries of 1915, for example, he writhed in writer's block. 'Again tried to write, virtually useless,' says one entry, followed two weeks later by, 'Complete standstill. Unending torments.' Shortly after that, it was, 'How time flies; another ten days and I have achieved nothing.'

Gustave Flaubert certainly would have sympathised. In a peevish letter to fellow writer George Sand in 1866, he wrote, 'My novel is going very badly for the moment . . . Ideas come very easily with you, incessantly, like a stream. With me it is a tiny thread of water. Hard labour at art is necessary for me before obtaining a waterfall. Ah! I certainly know THE AGONIES OF STYLE.'

For Flaubert, then, it was not just hard, but capital-letters hard – and he leant, albeit with a hint of bitterness, on a pal who understood. A century and a half later, the technology has changed but the feelings have not: my phone is full of text conversations with writer friends, confessing our nervous breakdowns back and forth. We say, 'Keep going.' We offer to read things. We console each other about unimpressed agents, stalled novels and crap money.

Parker's editor Covici had more than one writer to soothe; in 1951 he got a letter from novelist John Steinbeck. 'I feel just worthless today,' it said. 'I have to drive myself. I have used every physical excuse not to work except fake illness. I have dawdled, gone to the toilet innumerable times, had many glasses of water. Really childish.' This feebleness of morale is perhaps the main issue we all face: a writer can't rely on it from one week to the next. Just as we approach a tricky part of our manuscript and are most in need of our courage, it throws itself to the ground like a football player hamming up a minor injury. It can't go on. It's outraged by the scale of the challenge. It would rather die here than take another step across the page.

All good writers are also good readers, so comparison becomes a problem. You've read the greats and now you think you can write a book that should be sold alongside them? Who do you think you are? Looking at our bookshelves, it is difficult to see gaps that we might be able to fill with our own negligible experiences and abilities. Even if we start confidently, motivation drains away: often the first attempt is so poor that you wish you hadn't tried. It was so much better in your imagination.

It's not as though the pain is even over quickly, because writing a book is unbelievably time-consuming, and progresses incrementally as we labour over a seventh or eighth draft of the idea we came up with when our hair was darker and our cheeks not yet sunken. Usually it's badly paid, or unpaid, or done in the hope that payment may be offered later, even if only when we're dead.

One realisation has made all of this so much easier to tolerate that I only wish I'd accepted it earlier in my career: that every writer, however talented or experienced, finds the process hard. If you struggle to write, that says nothing at all about who you are – except that you're a person willing to engage seriously with a craft.

Another comforting fact: as I explained in chapter two, happy things can occur in your brain without your awareness. If you write, you may feel sometimes, like Parker, Steinbeck, Kafka and Flaubert, that your unsuccessful efforts amount to wasted time – but you'd be wrong. A writing problem that has driven you to lose sleep and berate yourself for months on end can quite unexpectedly resolve itself. Sometimes this brings a sudden feeling of lightness, which would be irritating if it weren't such a relief. You think you're stuck, but you're always moving. You're tunnelling, and eventually you'll see sunlight.

Maybe, bearing in mind the scale of the task, a little avoidance is understandable. Maybe we are wise to procrastinate before we write, unnecessarily reorganising a bookshelf, fetching another glass of water or, as a friend confessed the other day, reading about ants on Wikipedia. Once we're in the work, after all, it will ask so much.

I think writers need each other, just as people who believe in astrology or are passionate about trains crave like-minded souls and the warmth of human understanding. Every writer you love has persevered through all of this, and many of them are here in this chapter, ready to vent about what they find so tough, and to be believed, and to share useful advice and wisdom. If you're in the thick of it yourself, they might just get you through the pain threshold to whatever lies beyond.

Holly Bourne, novelist

I hate myself when I'm drafting. I turn into a horrible person. I'm distracted, I'm grumpy. My house falls apart. I smell.

It doesn't get easier, putting words on a page, and it's so much more fun to just open your fridge and look in it. Do you ever do that? Just go downstairs and waste five minutes of your life staring into your fridge?

My first drafts are garbage. I write them thinking, 'This is terrible. This is terrible,' and I know, intellectually, that I felt like this about all the other books when they were at that stage, but now they're all polished, published things on my shelf that I'm really proud of. I think, 'No, but maybe this one *is* rubbish.'

Even though I love my job, it's funny how much I hate my job.

Rumaan Alam, novelist

I used to work at *New York Magazine* editing the interior-design issue, which came out twice a year. There was a hiatus between issues, and I said to my husband, 'OK, I am going to write a book, but I have to finish it before I go back to work, so I only have twelve weeks.'

I laid out all these very complicated circumstances: 'I will write every night. You'll put the children to bed at seven o'clock, and I'm going to sit downstairs in the living room at this little table, and you cannot speak to me, and you cannot ask me what I'm doing. In the morning, you will have to get up with the kids but I will take them to school.' My husband is a good man. He said, 'OK, that's fine. I won't speak to you from seven o'clock for these three months.'

That's exactly what we did. I would work from seven until two, sometimes three in the morning. And then I would sometimes get up at six when the boys got up, feed them breakfast, take them to school, come home, fall asleep again, and then get up around noon. I would make dinner, get the house in order, pick the boys up from school, be with them through dinnertime, and he would put them to bed and I would do it all over again. It was extremely difficult, as you can imagine, but I produced a draft of the book in three months.

It sounds like you write very quickly.

Well, it's really important to point out that the relationship between a draft of a book and a finished book is not unlike the relationship between a seed and a watermelon. So when I talk about having a draft, what I have is a pile of grammatical mistakes, continuity errors, misspellings, illogical things, unfinished scenes and dialogue that leads nowhere. It's a disaster, but it exists.

What's the most challenging part of the writing process for you?

The entire task is a challenge. Landing on something that feels worth your time and worth your readers' time – that's not easy, because every story has been told. It's really simple to say, 'Oh, I'm gonna write a great family novel' – but then you read a Tessa Hadley and you're like, 'Shit. Well, she did it so much better, why would I even bother?' Or 'I want to write a novel that weds the political and the personal' – and then you read J. M. Coetzee and you think, 'Well, I can't do that.' Getting out of that headspace of comparison is not easy.

Being able to commit to a story, and see it through, is also challenging because it takes a long time. There's a lot of discipline involved in bringing it all together and making sense of it as a cohesive whole. That's hard work – but not in the way that being a nurse is hard work, so it's sort of difficult to complain about. It can be difficult to feel like the labour has been worth it, because it's just a private indulgence, until it's published and it becomes a public thing.

Will Harris, poet and essayist

My main experience of writing, and I'm sure this is true of most of us, is of constant shame, not being good enough and not having done justice to something. There's also a shame at the act of disclosure, which writing often involves.

John Lanchester, novelist and non-fiction writer

I started writing my first novel in 1990 and finished it at the end of 1994, and it was very stop–start. I kept losing confidence, and I still do. The main thing I learnt from that book was the importance of managing my mood swings, because I start writing with a sense of freedom and possibility, but I know I'm going to end up hating it.

I always have this metaphor in mind of what it's like to write a book. You see a natural feature like a wall or a rock formation that looks really pretty, and you go and have a look at it. You get closer, and there's something attractive and engaging about it, and you move slightly further in, and then you realise it's actually a cave-like structure, and it feels protective. You're inside this thing, and it's still beautiful and interesting, and you go a bit further and – oh. Actually, you realise, you're in a tunnel. Now the only way out is to go all the way through.

That's the writing process for me. At the beginning it's all possibility and openness, and 'Wouldn't this be fun?', and 'That's a good idea, how about adding this other bit?' There's a sense of play and freedom at the idea-having, note-taking, noodling-around stage, but once you get going, there's a point of no return where basically you have to finish it. I always end up hating the book, or losing confidence in it. Very often actually, the main symptom is a feeling of, 'This is the wrong book to be writing. That other idea I had is much better and I should've done that instead, but it's too late and I've got to press on.'

I spend a lot of time and trouble at the planning stage, and get as much of that work done in my head as I can, and I try to stress-test the idea and think it through, partly because I know that six months or a year into writing the book, I'll be thinking it's a mistake. While I'm still thinking clearly, I have to plan as much as I can. Then I have to ignore the mood swings, which are just part of the process, and keep going.

I remember having one of my patches of hating my first book and not working on it, and I made a deal with myself that whatever else I did, I would finish that draft. I hadn't told anyone except my wife that I was writing the book – so I told myself I didn't have to show it to a soul. I wouldn't necessarily try to get it published, but I would finish that draft. That was helpful, the commitment to – however I felt about it, whether it was a disaster or not – get to the end of a draft.

Remember that the thing that causes pain is wanting it to be good, and the truth is that you can't tell whether it is or it isn't when you're in the middle of it. You've got no idea.

Mhairi McFarlane, novelist

Something you learn to live with as a writer is that you're always practising. As a romantic-comedy writer, I used to have this feeling of, 'Oh, I'm going to ascend to a summit, where bestselling author Marian Keyes will give me my special cloak. There I'll be, and I'll know how to write books, and it'll be like a hot knife through butter every time' – but it never gets like that. Every single time I start to write a novel, I sit down and think, 'Oh my god. This is an absolute scam I've been running for years, and now I've got to pull it off again.'

Kiley Reid, novelist

If you're dreading writing a particular scene, I think that's because you shouldn't be writing it – or you shouldn't be writing it in the way that you've planned. Your first thought is not always your best thought.

Geoff Dyer, non-fiction writer and novelist

There is a pattern that I recognise now. I finished my last book a while back, and I was ecstatically happy during the last six months of writing it. I was putting in really long hours, and it wasn't requiring any self-discipline on my part, because it was all I wanted to do. So I made a resolution that I would do what I've never been able to do before: as soon as I'd finished that book, I would go straight on to the next book without a pause.

Then I failed to keep that resolution, and I fell into my normal pattern, which is to do nothing and become rather depressed. I wasted a lot of time before I properly got going on this current book, and even now, the contrast between those effortlessly long shifts that I could put in before and the kind of concentration I can muster now is considerable. I recognise this feeling.

Gradually, I would say two things are going on – one, the length of time I'm able to concentrate on this new book is increasing; and two, the amount of will that I'm needing to draw on, in order to get going on it, is reducing. Maybe the worst is over – the year that I spent doing almost nothing, just foolishly squandering my time.

One of the weird bits of self-discipline that I've needed to acquire is the capacity to not fall into complete despair during these long interludes when I'm not doing anything. The instinct is, of course, to think, 'I'm finished. I can't do it any more,' but now I'm so familiar with that feeling that I'm able to sort of ride it out, because I recognise that for me, this is part of the process. Each of my books is about something completely different to the previous one, and it has a form that is uniquely appropriate to that subject. I would almost go so far as to say that this period of not doing anything is a necessary part of decompression – so that I can start over with what is genuinely a new book.

Ruben Östlund, film-maker

When I'm about to direct a film that I've written myself, I get this great feeling: 'This is going to be so fantastic.' Then every day I go on set, and I feel completely devastated because it's so awful.

Cressida Cowell, children's writer and illustrator

Anybody who's a writer knows that it's emotional stuff. One minute you think, 'I'm a genius!' and the next minute you think, 'I'm an idiot!' – and the swing between those two can happen quickly, and that makes it very emotional. If you're writing stuff that is going to resonate with other people, it can be funny and dramatic and exciting – but it has to be meaningful, I think. So you're taking a lot out of yourself, and the temptation to put things off or to continually revise is a very strong one. I think it's been a real advantage to me to have always had an impossible deadline. I've never had enough time, and I might not have realised it then – when I had one, then two, then three babies, and the deadlines, and it was stressful – but there were some advantages to it. I had to do it.

John Crace, political columnist

The pressure of deadlines is the hardest thing about my job. My Parliamentary sketch goes up on the *Guardian* website on the night that I write it – but I have to work to a print deadline as well, because it appears in the newspaper the next day. During the COVID-19 pandemic, there would be a five o'clock press conference every afternoon, which would go on for about forty-five minutes – and then I'd have to write 800 words before 7.30 p.m. I had under two hours to distil the press conference, make sure that I had the right themes, and try to be funny about it.

I could often feel my heart racing. I would be panicking: 'Oh god, I've got to write, I've got to write! Help, help!' Sometimes I couldn't think of my opening, and I'd think, 'I've wasted fifteen minutes of two hours. That's an eighth of the time available, and I haven't written a word!'

Raven Smith, columnist and essayist

Even when I had my first deal, I didn't think it was possible to actually write a book. All I could think was, 'This is so hard! How do people do this? How can there be so many books in the British Library? Why doesn't everyone just give up?'

Sathnam Sanghera, journalist, novelist and non-fiction writer

I don't believe in writer's block, because I write for a living, and if I have writer's block, I can't support myself and I die. I think writer's block is something posh people have. 'Oh no, I can't write!' Well, you're going to starve then.

Do you go through tough patches, though?

Of course. At the beginning of a project, it could be anything – it could be brilliant. I think writing any project is a slow exercise in disappointment, in that it goes from being this infinitely clever idea to being a banal piece of writing with obvious errors and flaws.

What happens, though, is that when you give it to a reader, they get a sense of how you felt when you started the project. You only see the problems, but they don't. They see the initial promise and loveliness.

Maggie O'Farrell, novelist

Writing is graft, but enjoyable graft. I don't really understand the people who say, 'I hate it, it's so difficult, it's so awful, I'm so tortured.' I always think, 'Well – don't do it then! Go and do something else.' You've got a job where you can sit at home in your pyjamas talking to your imaginary friends – I mean how bad can it be, really? Try saying that to a coal miner.

Writing novels reminds me a little bit of bringing up children. Every child has his or her own joys and challenges, very peculiar to them, and I think novels are the same. I don't feel that I have one method that I could use to write any book. With every single novel, I have to reinvent how to do it; it needs to have its own process and its own way in, and its own rituals and research. I have a huge learning curve with each one.

For me, it takes the form of a wave pattern. You have a big upswing of optimism, excitement and inspiration, and you think, 'Yes, I love this idea – it's going to say everything I need to say.' You write and you write, and you get lots of words down, and then it's always followed by a big crash. For a couple of days or a week, you think it's all awful: 'I'm absolutely useless. I'm never going to finish this – it doesn't work.'

But you need that. You need the upswings in order to get words down, and then you need the terrible crash, because that's when you edit yourself. That's when you look at what you've written and think, 'That doesn't work, this whole structure doesn't work – but actually there's that one paragraph or chapter that I think is close to what I need it to be.' You have your creative optimism, and then you have your slash-and-burn week, and with any luck you'll have another upswing after that.

I hope I never think, 'I've written a book and it's perfect. It's exactly what I need it to be,' because I think that's the point at which I would stop. At the end of writing a book, even if I feel as though I've come close to what I set out to do, I always have a slight scratchy feeling of dissatisfaction with it. I always think, 'I did the best I could, but I didn't get to exactly where I needed it to be.' I think I need that slight sense of disappointment. That's what spurs me on to write the next book.

George Saunders, short-story writer

I've found that fear continues to be such a good friend to us as writers, because it's actually an aesthetic guide. When you start writing a book, you should be afraid that you're going to fail and bore the reader. Then once the story starts, it will present built-in difficulties, and the reader will understand that the whole purpose of the book is for you to overcome those difficulties.

I wrote this book about Abraham Lincoln, *Lincoln in the Bardo*. That's a big difficulty, to write a novel with Lincoln in it. When I was younger, I would have said, 'Oh, that's too hard, I can't do it – I might screw it up.' With a little experience you say, 'The thing you're afraid of is going to be the thing that you convert into a virtue.'

If you're afraid that your story is boring, then don't make it so boring. It sounds a little facile, but I always love that moment when I think, 'Oh my god, this story's going to be a disaster if I . . .' and then a little voice says, 'Well, don't do that.' How else can you succeed unless there's a high risk of failure? And the high risk of failure is also felt by the reader, I think. When Manuel Puig writes *Kiss of the Spider Woman* and we see that it's all going to be in dialogue, we think, 'Hmm, I don't know about that,' and he says, 'Well, let me prove it to you – let me show you that this is a good move.'

Any time you're in the middle of a work of art and it starts to resist you – that's great. The resistance is a sign of independence and power, and your job is to work with it. If you're writing a story that has no problems, you're not writing a story.

When you're stuck, there's a quick motion you can make that is so powerful. Very honestly ask yourself, 'What's the problem?' You can answer it very bluntly: 'It doesn't make sense that the dog could drive a car.' It's never anything too intellectual. Once you've turned your mind to the problem, I think you're already close to solving it. You're not despairing any more. You're just saying, 'Yeah, this thing I'm making has a technical problem. I don't see the solution right now, but that's OK. I'll fix what I can around the edges and maybe tomorrow it will come to me.'

There's a piece I'm working on now, and I have the worst kind of problem: it's about eighty per cent good. It's easy to go, 'Eighty per cent! Good enough.' But I know if I just bear down on it, I can get it a few points higher. For me, the trick at that point is to say, 'OK, something's wrong with this' and not to add, 'therefore I'm a loser' or 'therefore I should quit'. The story is a product of me, but it's not me, so just like when you see yourself in a home video, you know: 'Do I walk like that?' Well, there's walking like that being done, but it doesn't necessarily have to be an indictment.

Meg Mason, novelist

There's a quote on your website from Ian McEwan: 'Hesitation is essential to art.' What does that mean to you?

I think it's a lovely way of rebranding procrastination. I understand that procrastination is really fear – it isn't laziness. It's not that you're scared of the task itself or the work that's going to be involved, either; I think it's a fear of beginning it and having to see straight away that you're not equal to it. The idea of being confronted immediately by your own lack of ability is fatally off-putting.

I think, though, that describing it as hesitation says something about how seriously you're taking it. I'm hesitating because it's so important to me, and I value it so much, and I want to do it – and so of course I can't just blithely rush headlong into it. If you're cautious and a little bit anxious, that's probably a sign of how serious you are. I guess at some point, though, you have to decide to stop hesitating. He didn't mention that part. I wish he had.

Before Sorrow and Bliss, *you spent a year writing a novel that you then decided not to publish. Hearing that made me think about how hard it can be to walk the line between, 'My gut is telling me that this isn't working,' and 'Pull yourself together and keep going.' It must have been very difficult to know what to do.*

Exactly. If you've done any kind of writing before, or you just want it really badly, you accept that it is hard – but I became confused as to how difficult it should be, and the worse it got, the harder I tried.

When you've been a freelance journalist, you have a certain discipline. I thought, 'I'll just fall back on that and keep working.' If you're not the kind of person who shows your writing to anyone as you go along, you can end up on a year-long journey in the wrong direction. The longer you work on it, the greater your sense of sunk cost, and you can't bear to cut your losses.

As devastated as I was, I felt relieved as soon as I'd told my publisher that I didn't want to publish it. She was so clever in the way that she helped me through the next bit, letting me think I had quit writing novels permanently, which at the time I thought I had. I asked her recently, 'Did you actually believe that?' and she said, 'Absolutely not, because you can't help yourself.' That was her measure of a writer – we just can't help ourselves in the end. Even if you fail, and you've tried multiple manuscripts, if you keep coming back to it that ought to make you feel good. It's proof that you are a writer even if you haven't got anything published yet.

It's quite a neat story to be able to say, 'Oh, I wrote a thing that was terrible – and then I wrote *Sorrow and Bliss* and it went brilliantly and it was all worth it,' but it won't always be like that. I will write things that will fail after this, and there are going to be projects that don't get redeemed. I'll just have to find a place to put that, and a way to work around it and keep going.

What would you do differently if you found yourself struggling again?

I would try to reframe it. If I've spent six weeks on something that then grinds to a halt, instead of brutally punishing myself for the waste of time, I would try to say, 'Isn't that good? It only took you six weeks to work out that that's not the way to do it, and you're closer now to finding the right way.'

When I was writing *Sorrow and Bliss*, I felt very excited about it, but it never stopped being scary because I wanted it so much – so I got into this peculiar practice. At the beginning of the day, I would quickly write out everything that I was scared of: that it won't be good and that it will never be seen, or that it will be seen, or whatever it was that particular day. Then I flipped it around.

It sounds so odd but I started writing back to myself: 'Of course you're scared. Everybody would be scared in this situation. You did it yesterday, so now just do it today.'

That's not my natural way of being, but it seemed to work. I was at such a low ebb in terms of my confidence that one day, the only positive thing I could think of to put down on this list was, 'You've chosen a really good font.' I was scraping the barrel of ways to encourage myself, but gradually I saw some confidence return.

I say all of this knowing that writing a novel is not saving lives. I think if it's important to you, though, then it is a battle that you have to fight.

Brandon Taylor, novelist

I got a great piece of advice from a friend. I was really struggling to write, and he said, 'Brandon, why are you so afraid? It's just a draft. You know how to revise.' I feel like he put me on the horse when he said, 'It's just a draft,' and I've been on it ever since.

Just sit down and get the words out. It doesn't matter what it sounds like, or what it looks like. Let the words do what they will do, and believe in your ability to make more of them. There will always be more words.

Graham Norton, novelist

You got a two-book deal when you wrote your memoir The Life and Loves of a He-Devil, *and the second book was to be your first novel. Do you think it was helpful when you were writing the*

*novel to know that you had that deal in place, and somebody was
expecting something from you?*

It was more than helpful – it was vital. There was no way I'd
have finished that book if I hadn't been getting emails going, 'By
the way, where's the book?'

I remember I was in the office for *The Graham Norton Show*,
and I was talking about the novel and saying, 'God, I hope it's OK.'
One of the writers who works on the show said, 'Oh, you want it
to be good? Well, the thing to remember is, if you finish it, it is one
of the best novels in the world.'

That's true, because the vast majority of novels are still on
memory sticks or in the bottom of drawers or in people's minds.
Very few people get to write 'The End'. I interview writers, and
sometimes they say, 'Oh, I didn't get published until my third
novel,' and I look at them like, 'What? You wrote three novels?
Nobody was interested, no one cared, and you still managed to
write three of them?' I mean, that's incredible to me, and the ones
I'm talking to are those who did eventually get published. There
are probably people who are writing their eighth or ninth novel,
and no one's published them. But you know, they love it.

Emily St. John Mandel, novelist and screenwriter

How manageable have you found it to make a living as a writer?

To be absolutely candid, I am able to make a very good living
with literary fiction – but of all the writers I've ever met, I know
maybe two other people who can do that. I stand behind my
books, and I think they're good – but sometimes you write a book
that functions as a lottery ticket and behaves in the marketplace in

a way you would never have anticipated. That was *Station Eleven* for me.

That hasn't happened for the vast majority of novelists I know. Almost everybody is teaching or they're screenwriting – they have other things on the side. So I think you have to go into writing novels with the assumption that you will also need to do something else, and that is doable. I was an administrative assistant until a year after *Station Eleven* came out, and I was at peace with that. My assumption was that I'd be an administrative assistant forever and write books on the side. It would have been harder, but on the other hand, there's never enough time.

Meg Wolitzer, novelist

I'm aware that my attention has fragmented over the years, and I resent it, and I hate the fact that I have to think about it. I used to be able to read for many hours at a time, and that's harder now. Writing in my twenties was like when you see little children running: I want to run and run and run as a writer, and I can't always do that any more, and sometimes it's partly because I've sold my attention to the lowest bidder. To look at it another way, it's become harder to put myself in the little room of a novel, and stay there as long as I used to.

There's also how frightening and terrible so much of the news feels right now, and how much anguish we feel. We can draw from pain in our writing – but we can also be absolutely exhausted by it. Writing from anxiety seems to me a tremendously difficult thing to do. It can be the opposite of the freedom you need.

Still, writers scavenge without even knowing it. I have to take the long view, which is that the things I see and experience will go into work. They will contribute eventually to something that I want to say, something that I feel the need to say.

Anna Hope, novelist

It takes a huge effort of self-belief to write a first draft when you have absolutely no idea if it's ever going to get published.

Having been to Oxford University and studied the English Literature canon in the way that it's taught there, there's a whole anxiety of influence. There's a sort of brilliance that's really prized in places like that, and I'm not sure that's my way. There are very, very brilliant female writers, but for some reason I felt for a while that I was trying to please some sort of clever man, whoever he was. Maybe it was a male aspect of myself, but it was so liberating when I let go of that.

I did an event with a wonderful Oxford don recently, and he said that facility is the enemy. Part of me just crumpled up as he said that. I actually think that allowing yourself a certain ease in writing is hugely important. It comes down to being confident that you don't have to get it right the first time. If you get stuck, you can leave a note: caps lock, 'COME BACK TO THIS' – and it's really OK to push through. You have to not need it to be brilliant, because it's not going to be when it comes out. If I'm waiting for my work to be brilliant, then I get hidebound. I can't be that writer.

Elizabeth Day, novelist, journalist and non-fiction writer

You write in your memoir that when you were a feature writer at the Observer *and had published three novels on the side, your friend Viv told you, 'If you want to be Elizabeth Day, novelist, you have to see yourself as Elizabeth Day, novelist.'*

Yes, I think I'd always been a bit embarrassed of seeing myself that way, even though that's what I really wanted to do. At that time, I had been at the *Observer* for maybe six years, and it took me another two years to act on her advice – but I remember her saying that, and I also remember her introducing me to the concept of 'playing big'. It's the idea that, as women, we should claim the space; we should stop fannying around questioning ourselves and feeling imposter syndrome, because actually, a lot of the time we're already doing the stuff. We're doing it, and we should be treated on that basis alone.

I think those things are really important – you have to start by taking yourself seriously, and then other people will.

Sophie Mackintosh, novelist

I remember when I was at university, one of the creative-writing tutors talked to us about progression in your work: it's not always a linear, upwards trajectory. Often you're plateauing and feeling very disheartened – but there will come a moment, now and then, when you make a quantum leap. You don't know when that will be. Whenever I'm plateauing, I think about that and it gives me incentive to keep trying.

I think there's quite a lot of faith involved in writing books. Do you find that?

Completely. You have to believe in yourself in an industry that's really competitive. No one's going to cheer you on – you have to cheer yourself on and be good to yourself. That's why, when people do their own books down, I say, 'No, be proud of what you're doing.' It's very easy – especially, I think, as a woman writer – to be like, 'Oh, this little book? It's nothing. It's terrible.' I still fall into that trap. But no, it's a book. It's good. I wrote it. I should be proud of it.

4

How do we tell the truth?

'The job is to create a reasonable facsimile
of a human life, and that process is difficult.'

BRANDON TAYLOR, novelist

I recently heard the comedian Mike Birbiglia explain his philosophy on writing as follows: 'If you're not telling secrets, who cares?' He said this on his podcast *Working It Out*,* and I stopped chopping onions and made a note.

Unlike Birbiglia, I don't write for stage, but the test he implies with those seven words fits any kind of writing: it should always feel as though it gets at something true, and ideally something that has taken a little digging to reach. A writer can use all sorts of tools for that digging – empathetic imagination, academic research, personal reflection – but for me the main one has been interviewing. I vividly remember the first time I was allowed to do it, because I was euphoric afterwards; if the entrepreneur Lisa Hoffman were told today that Hattie Crisell remembers our interview this way, I suppose her reaction would be 'Why?' and also, 'Who?'

It was 2007. I was twenty-four years old. I'd recently got my

---

* Episode 111: 'Gary Simons: A New Comedian Asks Mike 10 Key Questions About Starting Out in Comedy'.

first journalism job as a magazine assistant. I was trusted to make rounds of tea, do administrative tasks and, on one occasion, brush the editor's hair (she had broken her arm). Outside of work I had a blog, mainly featuring anecdotes from my social life written in what I hoped was a wry tone. Thinking about it now makes me cringe so vigorously that I could shed my epidermis in one go.

That was my writing career, and I was desperate to move things along. I was always begging the editor for something more substantial, until eventually she agreed to let me do an interview for the beauty pages. Hoffman was visiting London to launch her skincare line and my editor was interested in her serums – but much more so in her long marriage to the very famous actor Dustin Hoffman.

I met her at a fancy hotel bar in central London. She was elegant and charming, and I was vibrating with nerves and excitement. The article was to be 600 words; that's about six paragraphs. I could have covered this with twenty minutes of well-managed conversation, but I didn't know that then, so I sat with her for hours, asking every question I could think of until I had enough material to write a book. I would spend the next two weeks trying to whittle my transcript down for the editor, who was disappointingly not as gripped by every line as I was. My main memory, though, is of that first sublime dopamine high of interviewing, which I still get today.

What is it that feels so delicious to me about an interview? It's the current between two people. It's the gradual revelation of intimacies, and glimpses of what makes somebody who they are: the truth of the interviewee comes into focus little by little, and I feel almost a change in the air as we start to understand each other. That can translate into something powerful on the page.

In the almost two decades that has followed, I've studied writing by doing it, reading it and taking a university degree in it – and the more I've learnt, the clearer it's been that truth is at the heart of all good work. This applies whether you're writing a historical novel or a zombie thriller, but it's a very particular kind of truth that I'm talking about, more feeling than fact. When writing feels true, the work becomes a surface that reflects and expands the reader's sense of what it is to be human. Empathy is always important, even if we're applying it to fictional characters. It is always the writer's job to think themselves into the heart of a situation, find the seed of something both familiar and new, and tease it into a story.

The piece I wrote about Hoffman was not powerful at all. It was flat and dull, bogged down in uninteresting detail and devoid of colour. It's a shame I didn't know how to write it, because I can see now the more engaging piece it could have been. I remember how she described herself at twenty-two, outside the law school with Dustin, the family friend who had become a Hollywood star. He took a break from filming in the early years of their relationship; he would pick her up from the library or bring dinner so she could study. This was the human story that she revealed over moisturiser samples, and I was touched, but I didn't know then how to turn a light on it.

Now I'd push gently at what it felt like to be the student falling in love with a famous actor, and how they created something so solid together. Did she take him to parties back then, and what did her peers make of him? Did fame make him more secure or less, and how did that alter him from the young man she'd known as a child? What has it been like to build their unusual life?

There is an art to asking. A good interviewer listens and is genuinely curious – and if the subject matter isn't particularly interesting, they work harder at being curious – but there's sideways work going on too. The questions aren't always the point. Sometimes they're a way of getting someone to unwind and give a clue as to what they feel strongly about, or to their vulnerabilities – to inadvertently tell their secrets, as Birbiglia puts it. Sometimes I ask something off-topic or share something of myself, because I've learnt that through authentic conversation, gems of unexpected truth can emerge.

Editing what I had more shrewdly – deleting most of it, in fact – could also have given me something that felt more truthful. The writer must direct an audience's attention to what's important: that's how they become a storyteller, as opposed to a disinterested recorder of information. Many of the non-fiction writers you'll hear from in this chapter have been diligent researchers, digesting millions of words from other people in order to write their own books – but they don't share that knowledge indiscriminately with the reader. Reality needs to be arranged and shaped so that it can come to life on the page.

You'll also hear from those who literally tell secrets in the form of confessional writing and know a thing or two about the pitfalls of that. There are fiction writers whose work opened up once they found a way to be more honest, and journalists who've become experts in drawing the emotional truth from their subjects, whether they're speaking to celebrities or war-zone survivors. The honesty of their work makes for satisfying reading, but I believe it also leaves us a little wiser than it found us.

Wendy Erskine, short-story writer

I know it sounds quasi-mystical that my characters come to me and reveal themselves, but it is a little bit like that. It is a process of trying to get to know who these people are and what they would do and say, and quite often, that doesn't come until I've drafted it quite a few times. There'll be times when I feel I've finally got to know a character, and when I look back at the beginning of a draft – I don't even mean a separate, earlier draft – I'll think, 'Never in a million years would they have said that. That's not them at all.' Then I rewrite it again.

I would say I do seven or eight drafts of most stories. It's funny, because in some ways, my style looks as though it's all put down without a lot of thought. Somebody once asked me, 'Oh, do you draft your work?' I think that they thought it was quite spontaneous, that I just dashed it off and that was it. There's that Dolly Parton quote, 'It takes a lot of money to look this cheap'; I honestly think with this type of writing, it takes a lot of work to make things look as though they are not highly wrought.

Your characters are so real. As a reader you get the sense that there's a whole world beyond what you're seeing in the story. I guess that comes from the weeks that you've spent getting to know these people.

I think that is part of the process, spending that length of time really thinking about them, and trying to get them absolutely in focus. It's funny what I'm trying to do, I think, because it's simultaneously trying to make these people very, very precise, but not so much so that readers can't project onto them. I rarely write a very detailed physical description of a character, because in some ways, that shuts readers out. The more specifics you give people, the less they supply their own ideas and their own aspect of the narrative. I think that's also why people take to my characters, because in a sense, they've often met me halfway.

Brandon Taylor, novelist

You wrote an essay for Literary Hub *called 'There Is No Secret to Writing About People Who Do Not Look Like You'. In it, you argue that writing about people of other ethnicities or other backgrounds comes down to empathy, and whether you can put yourself into somebody else's shoes – and that if you can't do that, then you shouldn't be writing at all. I found that such a useful way of thinking about character – through empathy.*

Thank you. When I write about black characters, that isn't easier for me than writing about white people, or straight people, or people who had money growing up. For me, the difficulty is the same, because in all of those instances, I'm having to enter into another person's life and to imagine for them a rich and full human experience, and that is difficult.

What frustrated me when I wrote that essay was that a lot of the discourse about writing across difference seemed to boil down to, 'Well, I'm black, so writing black characters is somehow easy, and you're white, and you can't, because you don't have that experience.' It feels like an excuse to say that, because it supposes that for the people with that lived experience, all they have to do is jot down what they did on Tuesday, and that is the extent of their craft. I just don't believe that. I think every writer sitting down to write well must begin with the question of other minds, and how you enter into them.

The job is to create a reasonable facsimile of a human life, and that process is difficult. It involves, I think, a fair degree of empathy and of really deep engagement with the matter of other lives. I take all of my characters so seriously, and I work so hard at my desk to make them feel full and human and real. That, to me, is what writing well is: can you create a real human experience for these characters, or are you relying on second-hand tropes and cardboard cut-out humans? And if so, why is that your impulse?

Mona Arshi, poet, novelist and essayist

Poetry has always been a vehicle for truth-telling, particularly when you think about barbaric moments of history – Second World War poetry, for example. I think a lot of that has to do with the fact that it doesn't tolerate clichés. Truth and untruths are really exposed in the very small space of the poem. Using the language of truth, for me, means avoiding sentimentality and familiar, lazy images. Images matter in poetry because they are freighted with meaning. When you resort to clichés it feels as if you're not trying hard enough to reach the truth, and you're settling instead on something that is familiar and is no longer doing the work of poetic language.

Jon Ronson, storyteller and author

You appear almost as a character within your non-fiction. It's quite an unusual approach.

That started because I just noticed that it was the easiest way for me to write a story, through the prism of my own experience. After a while I tired of it, and tried to write in different ways where I wasn't a character – and editors always told me to put myself back in there. Now I'm at peace with that.

There is a very funny bit in your book The Psychopath Test *– I suppose people would call this a faux-naive narrator—*

I'm going to interrupt and say that usually when I'm accused of faux naivety, what people don't realise is how genuinely naive I am.

Ha! Well, you write that A. A. Gill was once very rude about you in a TV review, and then you start speculating about whether he might have been a psychopath. It's very funny, but it also illustrates the larger point you're making in the book, that these diagnostic tests can make people go mad with their own power. Do you think that the narrator's voice you've honed helps you find a way in for the reader?

I do. I'm the reader, going into the situation with all of my own anxieties, issues and biases. I think a lot of non-fiction writers shy away from writing about their own biases, and they want to present themselves as figures of authority, but it's so much more fun to read, and just more true, if the narrator doesn't present themselves as a perfect being.

The memory that always pops into my head is of this TV presenter who was a little bit like me, and one time, he infiltrated the fashion industry. He had hidden cameras all over his body, and somebody gave him some cocaine. He went into the toilet and, in front of the camera, made a big show of opening up this little packet of cocaine and putting it down the toilet with this look of disgust. I watched it thinking, 'You work for the BBC. Don't tell me you've never seen cocaine before.'

What I don't like about that kind of piety and superiority is that it's not egalitarian, and I'm a believer in egalitarianism. It's hierarchical. I'm always suspicious of people like me who go into situations where the purpose is to present themselves as a representative of righteous society, while the other people are somehow lower in the hierarchy. I don't think it's what should be motivating the writer.

How do you navigate the moment when the people that you've written about read what you've written? There presumably are occasions when they are not thrilled with the outcome?

Yes, and it causes me a lot of anxiety. Then I think, 'Well, who am I writing it for? Am I writing it for the person being written about? Am I writing it for my readers? Am I writing it for society?' I have to balance those three things. In journalism, whenever you write about real people there is always that danger. I'm incredibly happy when I write something that the people in the book like, but when it doesn't happen – I guess if I feel I've been fair, then I feel upset that they're upset, but . . .

You can live with it.

Yeah. If I've been ethical, then I think, 'Well, I did what I could.'

Andrew Billen, journalist and interviewer

For an interview, there are three things you have to do. You have to think of good questions, put people in a frame of mind where they want to talk, and then find a way to write it entertainingly. You have a bit more discretion over the last bit and you can develop your own style.

I don't see any way around doing a lot of homework. I'm interviewing a comedian tomorrow and I'm trying to read both his autobiographies, even though it's only for a 1,400-word piece. That's partly to give myself confidence. It's so easy to find and read previous interviews online now; that means you know the interesting areas to ask about, but you also know the areas where he's said the same thing again and again, so you know what to avoid. Sometimes they're flattered if you know a lot about them when you go in. Often they assume that you do, and that you've read all their novels, so you don't want to piss them off by not having done so.

The idea that you can go in and wing it, having not watched the movie you're going to talk about, I find horrendous. I once interviewed Larry King, who did interviews incredibly successfully for CNN for decades, and he never did any research. I said, 'What do you do instead?' He said, 'I just ask, "Why?"' It was a good point, actually. 'Why?' is by far the best question.

You never know what the atmosphere is going to be like in the room – whether they're going to be hostile, chatty, suspicious, shy, over-talkative . . .

And sometimes the people who are going to be difficult have a reputation for that – so sometimes you're going in with anxiety about how it's going to go.

Oh god, yes. People sometimes ask if I get nervous before an interview. I'm always energised by meeting new people, but I am nervous about not getting anything good out of them, and twenty minutes in, I frequently have the horrible feeling of, 'This is all very well, but I haven't got anything. I'm going to have to get him or her off this topic and interject with a harder question.'

I don't believe in the Lynn Barber tactic of asking the worst question first, because I think that's going to piss them off and get their barriers up. How you make people talk, I think, is up to you, but I try to be a little bit conspiratorial, like we both know this is artifice, and a little bit humorous and ironic. Sometimes people don't get it at all, and then I go more straight, and ask, and be pleasant.

I've tried the other thing of being direct and tough, but there's absolutely no point in it. It will get you five or six paragraphs of sparky dialogue, but not the revelations and the intimacy that you really need. I've found generally, as I get older and maybe I care less about what people think of me, that I can ask the hard questions but in a soft voice – and often, I'll be quite surprised by the answer. If you don't ask about the delicate points in somebody's life, they're not going to volunteer anything.

Your editor at The Times *is Nicola Jeal, who has also edited me. One of the most useful things she said to me was, 'You have to ask the awkward question, and even if they don't answer, it doesn't matter, because then you've got some kind of response that you can work with.'*

That's very good advice.

I do hate it though when I have to ask questions that I know are unpleasant, and I can sympathise with why they won't want to answer.

But again, you can ask why. If they say, 'I really don't want to talk about that,' you can say, 'Why? Is it still very painful?' I suppose to a civilian, even asking the question sounds incredibly intrusive – but I think that when you don't, paying readers look at that article and think, 'Well, they didn't ask anything about his affair with so-and-so!' They feel diddled.

We're not there to make friends. Some journalists go in and they end up friends for life with a Hollywood star. I'm really not interested in that.

Will Storr, long-form journalist and author

In 2011, you travelled to Uganda and reported on the rape of men being used as a weapon of war. It's not an unusual occurrence and it's very under-reported, because there's stigma around it. You won the Amnesty International Award and the One World Press Award for that report. What are the particular challenges when you're writing about something so sensitive?

I did a lot of reporting in conflict areas, sometimes in war zones, with very traumatised people. It's obviously important not to pressure interviewees who might not want to talk about things for lots of very good reasons, including their own safety. The culture in Uganda is extremely homophobic. If you admit to being a male survivor of rape, people will accuse you of being gay, and in that part of the world if you're gay, you could be ostracised, beaten up or even arrested. One of the guys who had been repeatedly raped was thrown out of his home by his wife. The doctor would give him only a paracetamol for his very injured body, so it was really a terrible situation. What was inspiring was that despite the stigma, when we turned up at the Refugee Law Project in Kampala, there was a queue of men waiting to speak to me.

The most powerful lesson that I took from that work is that there's a tendency among liberal Western people to accidentally patronise people who live in African countries and have had these kinds of experiences. There's this narrative of, 'Oh my god, they're so brave, they're so amazing, they're so wonderful,' and we all want to say these things and believe that they're true, but I think that's dangerous, because it others them. They become, in a way, angels that are elevated from human experience and suffering, where in reality they're ordinary people in a great deal of pain. So there's a temptation to go into the interviews all smiley – 'Hi, how are you? Oh, thank you so much!' – but I was very conscious that I would talk to everyone in a straightforward, adult way.

The report that you wrote is graphic and upsetting, but the conversations would have been much longer and more numerous, and that's difficult material to look at in depth. What was the effect on you as the writer?

I suppose the answer I'm supposed to give is, 'It was really traumatic' – but I didn't find it traumatic. I found it fascinating. When I was doing the interviews, I felt it was important to present an atmosphere of safety to these people. You don't want to be crying in front of them. It's professional, dignified, supportive and friendly, but not emotional. Then my head would be full of the story, the arrangements, the things falling through, the photographs, so it's only when I'd get home that I'd really process it. My wife would always say that three or four days after I got back, I would have an angry meltdown at some poor waiter – it would come out in a weird way. So I think it did affect me, but my number one concern was the story.

I haven't been to areas of conflict, but I have interviewed people who've been through terrible experiences, and I think the least a journalist can do is be willing to calmly bear that conversation with someone, if they're willing to have it. It's much more difficult for them.

Yes, I think what's much more valuable than weepy sympathy is giving people respect and a sincere thank you, and doing honour to their story. I did sense sometimes that the charity facilitating the meetings felt discomfort with the questions that I would ask; you'd always want the detail, because that's what made the story come alive. I would say, 'It's up to them. They're an adult with agency, just like any pop star that I might be sent to interview in Los Angeles. They've agreed to the interview so I'm going to ask them the question, and if they don't want to answer, that's completely fine.' Nine times out of ten, they did want to answer, and I think part of what made that sexual violence story so impactful was the detail that the interviewees granted me in those conversations.

You've explored vulnerability of different kinds through your whole career. You've also written very personal things about your own life. Do you find that difficult?

No, I find it easy. I went through a phase of endlessly writing confessional things for the *Guardian Weekend* magazine. I don't know why, but I find it much easier to talk to the screen or page than to people in real life, and I've always thought that when you're writing about yourself – if you're not really willing to go there, then what are you doing?

One of the big formative moments for me was as a young writer reading Blake Morrison's *And When Did You Last See Your Father?* In that book he describes having a bath as an adult in his childhood bathtub, and he masturbates, and he describes the sperm in the water. It is shocking but I thought it was absolutely brilliant – that in this very literary memoir about the life and death of his father, he had the courage to really go there. I was hugely impressed by that.

My phase of confessional writing stopped, however, when I encountered the phrase 'sad fishing'. Confessional writing has become a way of grabbing at status in our very modern, social-media world. I think it's something I'll go back to as I get older, but at the moment, I'm stepping away from it because it has started to feel a bit cynical: 'Look at all my wounds. Look at all my wounds. Buy my book!'

Ruben Östlund, film-maker

I want to have a sociological approach to film-making; I want to look at how a situation can create a certain kind of behaviour. In the times we live in, we are completely obsessed with the individual – we're trying to seek the answers in a good guy or a bad guy. I'm much more interested in the approach of sociology, because it doesn't put blame on the individual – it tells us something about the context, and how it would be possible for us to end up doing the same thing.

I try to approach my films like that. I want to find a dilemma that the characters are dealing with that is easy to identify with. You have two or more options, and none of them are easy, and all of them are going to have consequences. I love it when that happens in normal social encounters, and all of a sudden we're faced with doing something that is morally wrong. Then we can really relate: 'Oh my god, maybe I also would have done this.'

I'm very interested in when we fail. I'm not so interested in when we succeed in being good.

You are the writer but also the director of all your movies. I wonder how much those two roles can be separated, and how much it's part of the same job of creating a vision.

The great thing about being the director is that I can add to or take things out of the screenplay, because it's my own text. I get my actors to improvise during casting, and if they say something great then I put it into the script. Then on the shooting day, when we're first trying out the scene, I want them to be free. Even if we know exactly where we're coming from and where we're headed and they have gates that they have to pass through during the scene, they are free to relate to the situation as they would as human beings.

I ask them, 'Do you believe in the behaviour that I have written down here?' Sometimes they say, 'No, I would never do this,' and then I get super interested. I say, 'Why? Can we change something in the set-up, so it's possible for you to do what it says in the script?' I'm trying to capture something that feels true and not constructed, and it's an important part of the writing process.

John Lanchester, novelist and non-fiction writer

If you ask people where the word fiction comes from, they think, oh, I don't know, Latin *fictio* meaning 'make shit up'. And it's not. It's the past tense of the Latin verb *fingere*, which means 'to shape', like shaping things on a potter's wheel. Fiction is shape and structure.

I've written five novels, one book of short stories and four works of non-fiction, and I learnt a lot about how to tell non-fictional stories by writing novels. My first book-length work of non-fiction was a memoir called *Family Romance*, about my parents. They had complicated lives in various ways. They had both died by the time I had children, so in case my kids got curious about what their grandparents were like, I wanted there to be a record of it.

I was very conscious of wanting to answer the question 'What were they like?', and to convey that feeling of what someone was like, I found I had to do an extraordinary amount of selection and omission. There's not a sentence in that book that is made up, but there's a tremendous amount of shaping, and in that sense 'fiction', in order to tell the truth. Character is really about where you choose to put the spotlight. I carried that lesson from fiction to non-fiction, and then from non-fiction back to fiction.

As for novels, you can do pretty much anything in terms of flights of fancy – there's a novel by John Updike where the characters swap race and swap sex halfway through – but it has to feel true. There are no rules other than that. The thing is, life is full of events that don't feel true but have actually happened. Life's full of incredibly unlikely and implausible events, and things that you don't want to believe. The funny thing is that in fiction you can't write about unlikely things, because the reader will reject it – they want it to have that feeling of veracity – whereas in non-fiction, the fact that something actually happened in the world justifies you including it. Unlikeliness is the secret weapon of non-fiction, whereas fiction has a sense of infinite possibility, but also this very unforgiving rule that it has to feel true.

Georgia Pritchett, screenwriter

Comedy is as much about the jokes you don't use as the jokes you do. It's so easy to think, 'Oh, that's a funny joke, I'll keep that in,' but if it doesn't come from character or truth, then it's not helping the script. Being strict with yourself and being brave enough to make everything authentic is really important. It makes a huge difference to the end result.

Curtis Sittenfeld, novelist

You don't shy away from sex scenes, and I think you write them very well. What do you think they bring to a story?

I think the writer should do what the novel calls for. All my novels show people in a very intimate way, so it would be very plausible that I would show a person brushing their teeth or making a grocery list, or just sitting on the toilet – the things that people do in the course of a day. If there's a romantic relationship, the question to me is not 'Why would you include sex?' but 'Why wouldn't you?' I think it comes from a few impulses in me, but one is giving a comprehensive sense of what it's like to be this person.

Some people, I think, may be different in bed than they are out of bed. Are they more confident or are they less confident? Can they feel really close to another person or are they distant? I think reading about sex often makes people think of their own sexual experiences, or lack thereof, or experiences they wish they'd had, so it's a conversation between the reader and the writer.

I know I am opening myself up to mockery. There are those awards given annually for the worst sex scenes, which I think is a really ungenerous, shooting-fish-in-a-barrel—

I agree. It's so mean.

It's like giving an award for clumsiest person or messiest hair. I know that there are people who will think my sex scenes are inappropriate, they'll think they're cringe-inducing, but I think they serve a purpose and add something to the novel that can't be added in a different scene. So OK, opening myself up to mockery is the price I pay for writing the book the way I want to write it.

If you polled the reading population and said to them, 'You could read this novel and there'll be explicit sex, or there won't be explicit sex,' I think probably seventy-five per cent of people would be like, 'Put that explicit sex in there!' The people who don't like it are more vocal than those who do. But it's not for sales. I just feel like it belongs there, in depicting the totality of the character's life.

Mhairi McFarlane, novelist

You write romantic comedies where the love interests are just as fleshed out as the protagonists. What makes for a leading man who feels credible and real?

Give him his own point of view. There's nothing worse in a romance novel than when it's just Mr Tall, Dark, Handsome, and you don't know anything about him. He's a projection of female fantasy, but he doesn't have his own personality. What is he feeling? You should have that in your head every time he walks into a scene with your heroine, even though it's not on the page.

I also think that he's got to be funny. It works really well when he sees the absurdities or the contradictions in your heroine, so he can call her out on certain things, and obviously, she can call him out just as hard in return. But he's really got to come out of his corner fighting a bit, I suppose, and I think readers respond to that. They don't want Mr Nicest Guy in the Room. He doesn't ring true.

Listening to you, I keep thinking about Mr Darcy in Pride and Prejudice.

Yes! And obviously, Elizabeth and Darcy both suffer pride, and they both suffer prejudice. It's not 'Here's an angel meeting a bad man, but she converts the bad man to being nicer.' It's 'What do these two people learn about each other and themselves in conflict?', which is so appealing and satisfying. There are things about Darcy that are bad, that he will work on in light of his love for Elizabeth – and there are other things she got wrong about him. That's very satisfying, the balance of confusion versus enlightenment. I don't think it would ring true if it was just, 'I thought this person was awful, but it turns out they are great.' That never happens in real life.

Kiley Reid, novelist

When it comes to memory, you don't have to always tell the reader exactly how something happened; you just have to show how it happened for these characters.

Zoe Williams, journalist

For long periods of my career, I've written confessional columns, and I have one now. It's more difficult at my current stage in life, because you can't really write about your kids. You can't disclose much; you can't do the kind of thing that's going to embarrass them if their friends read it, because you know one friend always will, and show it to all the others . . . so basically, you're reduced to calling your husband an idiot, or saying something funny about your mother and hoping she's having a bad eyesight day, and that's it.

But over the years you've written very personal stuff. Why do you think that works for you?

I find it really, really cathartic. For me, it's a process of fucking up and atoning in public. If there's anything in my life that I feel bad about or think I did wrong, I can craft it into something readable and say sorry at the same time.

I feel sometimes that writing is a cheap form of therapy: you get to think it through, make sense of it, put it into words.

Exactly, and I think you can go really wrong with that and be way too disclosing. I have done that. I had a blog for *Marie Claire* at the beginning of the internet, and they wanted something like 300 words a day. This was before we really understood how the internet worked, and there was a sense that you had to fill it. I was writing really personal things and at one point I described an argument I'd had with my sister, and she saw it and got really angry with me. We had a massive row. I said, 'Oh, it's just my process – it's my life, I'm allowed to do what I want.' She said, 'Who do you think you are?'

Is it important to work out what's your story to tell and what is someone else's?

Well, I interviewed Jonathan Franzen once when he'd written a memoir about his siblings. I was amazed at how detailed he was, and I pointed out to him that each member of the family is going to have a different memory, which is going to intersect with another person's memories in a different way – so him accruing to himself the power to tell it is audacious.

He said, 'I present evidence of their lack of rage as a form of character witness on my behalf. If I were a jerk, they would be mad at me.' I thought, good answer. So I plead the Franzen here. If I were a jerk, people would be angrier with me.

David Sedaris, essayist and performer

Some time after my sister Tiffany killed herself, another of my sisters, Amy, told me she'd been to see a psychic, and I wrote an essay about that called 'The Spirit World'. I read the essay out loud, and it worked but the ending wasn't quite there – and so, as I often do, I threw away the last two pages and tried again.

When you're writing about your life, there are so many bits to choose from. The story of me dealing with my sister's death hasn't ended; there will be more to it next week and the week after that. What happened when I had a second try is that I wrote something that I never wanted anyone to know, because it really makes me look bad. It was about the last time I saw Tiffany: she came to a show I did in Boston, and she came to the stage door, and I had the stage manager close the door in her face.

It was not easy dealing with Tiffany. She was a mess, and it could take you weeks to recover from an encounter with her. She could say really hurtful things, or she could tell you something that would make you so angry or sad. I couldn't have a conversation with her and then go on tour for another four weeks. I didn't intend never to talk to her or see her again, but that's what happened. I never spoke to her or saw her again, because she killed herself.

I didn't mean to tell that to the world, but I did. I got a lot of letters afterwards that said, 'I don't even want to read your books again – you're a monster.' But I got an equal number of letters from people who said, 'I have a Tiffany in my family, and I know exactly what you mean.' Those letters meant more to me than the ones from people who didn't have a Tiffany in their life but were judging me.

That rewrite made it a better essay, because I was completely naked. I'm never going to write about what I do in the bathroom, and I've never written an essay in which I'm having sex – but when I rewrote that essay about Tiffany, I felt like I peeled something away. That's always what you want.

Grace Dent, restaurant critic, YA writer and memoirist

You have to be unafraid to say things that reveal how you actually feel. I think that's where my writing really took off – the moment

I started to reveal that I don't think I'm very beautiful, that I think I've got awful teeth, and that my bum is always far bigger than I want it to be. Once I started to be a little less general and a bit more real, I think that's when people started to properly read me and warm to me.

When I decided to write my memoir *Hungry*, I knew that my relationship with my parents would be a big part of at least the first half, because it's about growing up, food and nostalgia. The second half was really difficult, though, because I had a choice to make: whether or not to mention that my dad had developed dementia. I could have left it out. I could have made the second half a triumphant *The Devil Wears Prada* or *Ugly Betty* story where, despite everything, I rise through the ranks of media, and isn't everything great? I could have just glossed over the fact that for the last ten years, I've been going back and forth to Cumbria and dealing with losing my dad.

In the end I thought, 'The truth is actually interesting, and it's fighting to get out.' I knew it would cause problems, but I chose the hard route.

I remember when things first started to get really bad, say, nine years ago. Week by week, I used to think, 'If we just get through this bit, then I can go back to being me.' I don't have children, but I should imagine that this is what it feels like when you have a baby. Then bit by bit, you realise that you'll never be that person again. I'm never going to be the woman I was before I made the decision to go home and look after my dad and lose him in front of my eyes. I suppose what I'm saying is that I had to write about the realities of dementia. I don't think that what I've been through is remotely unusual. There are millions of people right now going through exactly this with a parent, or people who've already been through it. It's pretty hard, and there's so much that I've left out of the book – but even so, I was dragging my family into a spotlight. Did they want it? I don't think so.

It has been bizarre to release it into the world because I get messages non-stop, every day, from people who've been in the same position. It's not snuggly and lovely – it just feels like it's real, and I have done something that is actually good. People get in touch and say, 'Thank you for making me cry. I've needed that cry for four and a half years.' They'll say, 'Thank you for writing that line where you said, "I won't talk about the things that happened before my dad had to go away, because it was not him – but all I'll say is that when I left him in the room, and he was crying, with me promising that I'd come back for him, it took away a bit of my heart that'll never grow back."'

That wasn't creative writing. That's the kind of thing that I would have written on a Post-it note and left for my partner to explain what I'd done that day. It's like your heart keeps growing a scab, but then every time you think it's OK, it bleeds again.

I think I've done something quite profound, because I've created a tidal wave of grief and suffering and understanding and love and warmth that is now coming at me all the time. I don't really know what to do with it.

Wendy Cope, poet

I dedicated my first collection to my psychoanalyst, because he helped me to get in touch with feelings I didn't know I had. I believe that some writers, such as T. S. Eliot and D. H. Lawrence, have looked into the possibility of psychoanalysis and decided it might destroy their creativity. You'd have to ask them why, but

I think maybe it's to do with the feeling that creative people are a bit mad. What I think is, I don't see how understanding more of the truth about yourself could make anyone a worse writer. It also overestimates the power of psychoanalysis, because I'm still quite neurotic enough to get by as a poet even after ten years in analysis – but it certainly made me less depressed and more confident.

Someone once fixed me up on a blind date with a psychologist, and almost as soon as we got together he was saying, 'Oh, psychoanalysis doesn't work, it's well known.' I thought, 'Well, this is obviously not for me.' There was not a second date.

George Saunders, short-story writer

You hoped initially to write like Ernest Hemingway, and then at some point realised that it was better to sound like yourself. I think so many aspiring writers have these moments of, for example, 'I would love to be Zadie Smith. I'm not Zadie Smith, I am never going to be able to write like her, so what is the point of me even writing anything?'

Yeah, and I think it's good to feel that way. First, everybody should want to be like Zadie Smith – but also if you have that feeling, it means that you love good writing, and you've established part of your lineage, and that lineage includes Zadie. I don't know a good writer who hasn't been in that position of admiring someone so much that they want to become that person. That's a sign of love for the form.

Then there's a bittersweet moment where you realise that if you set about being Zadie, or William Faulkner, or Toni Morrison, then you can only kind of be an assistant. You're never going to be more Zadie than Zadie, that's a given. Then furthermore, there's a moment where you realise that that particular voice, whoever your hero is, can't get into the space about which you know something unique. Even if you're only twenty years old, your life has given you certain gifts, hardships and insights that are not describable in anybody else's mode. In my case, I know some things about class and I know some things about work, and I didn't really plan to talk about those things in my writing. I was going to talk about trout fishing and being incredibly handsome – but I noticed that my prose lights up when I write about class, or when I write in a certain mode, or when I feel a certain way when I write. If the prose lights up, you have to go in that direction.

It's disappointing because you're leaving Zadie or Ernest behind – but it's also thrilling. For the first time, I saw a trace of myself on the page, and a trace of someone new.

Then the next turn of the mind is to say, 'OK, this first indication that I have some originality is pretty pathetic, but if I keep gnawing at it, maybe in time it will grow into something substantial.' I think that's just the way it goes, and I see it with my students. They come in and some of them are very adept impersonators. The job then, hopefully very gently and through line edits, is to show this person that their imitation of David Foster Wallace is not David. Sometimes if you do that, just by editing the lines, they start to sound more like themselves, and the beautiful thing is that a person who hits that place where they sound like themselves often recognises it and rejoices in it, and then your work is done.

Meg Wolitzer, novelist

As a reader, when you find something in a book that's off, you can lose a little faith in the writer – and that's the last thing I want for my novels. I want to fill in a world and make it very particular, but I don't want anything to stop the reader, for them to question it or have to go to Google. There's something very reassuring about kicking back and letting the writer be an authority – so I always want to make sure that my sense of things feels right.

Elif Shafak, novelist

Several political and social issues are woven into your work – freedom of speech, feminism, LGBTQ+ rights . . .

Yes, I think it's deeply tied up with the way I perceive the world. For me, writing has always been about paying more attention to the periphery than to the centre. I'm interested in stories, but I'm equally interested in silences – people who have been disempowered, disadvantaged, pushed to the margins of society, whose stories have been forgotten, erased or distorted. There's a part of me that wants to change the power ratio.

There's also, I think, the fact that I was in academia for many years and I love interdisciplinary work. I love reading philosophy, cultural history, cookbooks, political science, neuroscience – and learning is important to me. I've never been a big believer in that horrible distinction of highbrow literature versus lowbrow literature, either – I've never understood what that even means. Who decides? As long as it speaks to you in that moment, you can read anything and everything.

I feel very sad when I hear readers say, 'I read politics, history, philosophy and finance – but I don't have time for fiction. My wife reads fiction.' Those people don't understand that in the world of fiction, there's everything. We need to read both fiction and non-fiction, and disciplines that we know nothing about. Those are the fields that really nourish our intellect.

Reading your novel The Island of Missing Trees, *it struck me how painstakingly researched it was, not only in terms of the conflict in Cyprus, which is one of the themes of the novel – but also there's a huge amount of very specialist information in there about nature, insects and trees. How important is research to your fiction – and when you're doing that breadth of reading, is it difficult to whittle it down to what will serve the story that you're trying to tell?*

Yeah, I think for a long time you feel lost inside this massive sea of knowledge. What guides me is almost a childish curiosity. Writers should never lose that habit of asking small questions about big things: 'Why is it like that? What's the story behind that?' I mean, the books that I'm reading are so eclectic. One week I can read very extensively about butterflies, the next week, maybe sewage systems in Istanbul. They're completely unrelated, but in my mind they come together, and if the story takes me into a field about which I know nothing, I am ready to learn as much as I can.

Jesse Armstrong, screenwriter

In screenwriting, professionalisation can be a trap. You want to be a real writer, so you read a lot of screenplays and you watch a lot of movies, and that can take you further away from the truth rather than closer to it. You learn about structure, which is useful and necessary, but you get this glib relationship to the truth. You start to feel that the truth will stop you from having a cool arc, or from getting to the great bit of story that you want to write. I think you have to really beware that.

My way to work is to ask, 'What would this really be like?' Even if you're writing a superhero movie, the fun of it is, 'What if this unreal thing was real?' Therefore the way to make it engaging is not to think of the craziest power or laser or disaster that can happen, but to try to make it feel as it really would if you were able to shoot web out of your wrists. I think that's the feeling the audience want from a superhero movie, as well as some fights and so on. That's the emotional thing that I'm always driving towards.

Why do you think we want that, as readers or audiences?

As human beings we're all just hunting around trying to figure out what the fuck is going on. It's a great relief and pleasure to realise that someone else is having the same apprehension of the world as you are. That's why a good observational comic is very pleasurable to listen to, because you're realising that we all feel the same about something – and the smaller and more generally unnoticed it is in the culture, the more of a relief it is. The same thing goes for an observation by George Eliot or Tolstoy. We think of those writers as looking for their observations about the nature of existence or social relations on a high level – but I think a lot of the pleasure that readers get is actually more about what it feels like to walk into a room, or what it's like to be in a complicated emotional relationship with another human being. That's the texture that gets you through page by page, and makes a show enjoyable, scene by scene.

5

What shape is a story?

'Always write with an eye forward and backwards.'

ANDRÉ ACIMAN, novelist, memoirist and essayist

I have attempted to write several books before this one. I wouldn't say they're all dead, but they're certainly sleeping well.

Before I started trying, almost everything I'd written had been of fewer than 2,500 words. When I turned to books, what I discovered is that structure gets exponentially more difficult, and also more crucial, as the form becomes longer. It's the difference between building a functional cardboard box and building a functional skyscraper.

To labour the metaphor: a long story needs complex engineering. If the writer does their job, this effortful process should be hidden from the reader, which I think is why so many people are shocked by how difficult it is to write a novel. The organising and pacing that turn events into a meaningful story take deep thought and a lot of time, and when my author friends feel defeated by their latest projects, it's usually structure that is causing their anxiety. Until you land on the right shape for a book, it can seem as though there is no possible answer – because you're trying to solve a puzzle that doesn't yet exist.

Plot and structure aren't quite the same thing, but the former won't land unless you get the latter right. You could summarise a plot in a sentence or two: it's the stuff that happens in your story, and in a piece of non-fiction that isn't led by narrative, perhaps you'd call it the argument or the information. Structure, on the other hand, is how you deliver that plot or argument, and it makes all the difference between a successful story and a useless one. The goal is usually to transmit a certain experience to your readers in shades of fear, amusement or pathos – and to do that, you have to arrange the right points in the right order, and lead them smoothly along that path.

Different types of writing call for different structures. When I went to work at *The Times* in 2017, I'd already been a journalist for many years, but I felt very green in the merciless world of a newsroom. In my first few weeks, my editor's feedback was usually, 'Delete the intro and get to the point.' That's what I learnt from this most efficient medium: tell the reader what you're doing, and get on with it.

Later I took a screenwriting course. My first attempt at a few scenes revealed that screenwriting absolutely isn't journalism. My tutor had to explain that in TV or film, the writer's primary job is not to make what's happening immediately crystal clear. It's to plant clues, often more in stage directions than in dialogue, and if they do that skilfully then the audience can put together their own satisfying take on events over the course of an hour or two, without feeling they've been told anything. This means employing a different tone, but it also requires a more restrained and unfolding structure, and not always explaining the conclusion on page one.

There are templates for this stuff, most of which are variations on Aristotle's three-act framework: beginning, middle, end.

In class, I was taught about how this is usually interpreted in Hollywood. Act One: the protagonist loses control of some aspect of their life, and an inciting incident alerts them to the fact that a problem must be solved or a duty done. Act Two: the protagonist struggles with the challenge, and with the stakes rising we fear they are doomed. Act Three: the protagonist regains control, but not necessarily in the way they had hoped or expected; perhaps they learn something.

Lots of writers discard this prescriptive thinking, which they believe limits creativity and suffocates originality, and there are plenty of films that are shaped differently or in which the three-act arc is well concealed. Still, it takes skill to diverge from convention and pull off a good story. My tutor argued that even screenwriters who reject the template are often, to some degree, unconsciously following it. It's what the human brain expects a story to look like, so we all walk away feeling that the puzzle pieces have found their right place.

In this chapter, you'll hear from Swedish film-maker Ruben Östlund, whose movies are exhilarating in part because they resist a Hollywood shape. There are also novelists, journalists and a stand-up comic, each with their own take on crafting the perfect story for their medium. Some have props that they find helpful: essay plans, spreadsheets, test audiences, and sometimes even formulas. Alongside the technical talk, though, they come back repeatedly to feeling and rhythm, instinct and pleasure, and above all, satisfaction. We know a good story shape when we see it, because we're audiences and readers as much as we're writers. The work may be engineering, but ultimately it feels like chemistry.

Jesse Armstrong, screenwriter

Structure is the most difficult part of storytelling.

I internalised the feeling of a half-hour comedy from writing so much *Peep Show*, and other sitcoms too, and now even when I'm writing an hour-long episode, I think of it as a longer half hour. Anything you can do to make the rhythms of a structure feel natural to you is great, whether it's working on a soap or a radio show. Failing that, just watch a lot of existing shows or films, especially ones that you like.

Could you describe what those rhythms are, and what you're thinking about in terms of structure as you write?

What does it need to be a satisfying story? That's the great question, isn't it. I think what I need quite early on is an ending. When we start a writers' room, I'm quietly trying to edge us towards deciding on the ending of the season, and to a lesser extent on the ending of the show. Similarly, for an episode that we're starting to write, I want to know what end points we are aiming for.

After that, you just need to be interesting. I used to write on *The Thick of It*, and when Armando Iannucci was analysing a script he would say, 'There need to be more explosions.' Similarly, Stanley Kubrick would talk about 'non-submersible units' – I guess in both cases, they mean the good bits. You're going to need a bunch of good bits. I tend to think, 'What are the comic scenes that are going to get us through?' – and hopefully in the end, every scene will feel like that.

As we made more and more of *Succession*, what I realised is that comedy, in the way that I conceive it, is really synonymous with a twist or a tension. The scenes that are comic don't need to produce a laugh, and often don't in that show – but there is an irony, a contradiction in the very fabric of the scene that needs to be resolved. Drama writers say that every scene needs a 'turn'. I guess a scene can turn by someone coming in and saying, 'The White House is on fire – we need to scramble the jets!' But I would also want there to be a comic dimension to that scene. Where's the most interesting place for that to happen? Is it a kid's birthday party, where they're not thinking about national affairs? What about if we discover it at the lowest possible echelon of the fire service? What about if they're in a car where there is no opportunity to influence events? What if their phone is out? A classic Hollywood version would be that your husband or wife works for the Air Force and you've got a personal connection to these bigger events. That's the tension, and it's quite a big, simple, available one – but often the big, simple, available ideas are worth doing.

Then if you think of a three-act structure, I'm drawn to the feeling that at the end of the second act and beginning of the third act, you're at a moment of maximum crisis or complication. You're in a real pickle. Things are bad, and they get worse, and then they're really, really bad. I also love an episode that starts with an explosion or a moment of high complication, so I don't have any rules – but it would be very unusual for me to endorse an episode in which the final fifteen minutes had a meditative atmosphere. I want a sense of urgency.

Meg Wolitzer, novelist

I never begin with plot. I would never be able to say, 'This should happen and this should happen,' until I knew who the characters were. How would I know what they would do? As a writer, I don't want to be the child pushing around little Lego figurines – that would be about me and my desire, rather than the characters' desire.

I have something that I jokingly call my eighty-page plan. I start each novel by writing roughly eighty pages without worrying about what genre it is, whether it will be published, or whether people will review it well. Then I print it out, preferably in a different font – Palatino makes mediocre work better – and I go and sit somewhere new to read it. I really start to reckon with what I've done, and I see what it is. That's the moment when I organise the book.

I make a kind of emotional outline. 'This section is the part where she really grieves her brother's death.' There's plot in there too. Then I'll get excited about a turn: it can be so exciting as a reader when something shifts and it feels earned. I don't want you to think I sit here constantly excited as a writer – mostly I'm just studiously watching, and changing, and getting rid of, and trying to plug those holes. But eventually, a plot rises up from the seeds of all the things that you've put in.

Are you consciously thinking, 'This protagonist sees it one way at the beginning of the book, but they're going to have a different perspective at the end of the book', or are you just letting that happen?

For the first draft, I'm trying to let it happen – and anyway, maybe there's no change. You have to be willing to let your characters be who you've come to know they are, and sometimes that involves them not changing even though it might feel rewarding if they had. I don't want to foist epiphanies on them.

And if you're foisting an epiphany on a character, you're also foisting it on the reader.

Exactly. Let people try to understand it themselves. The beauty of fiction for me comes from the links between parts of it – you think about something that happened earlier in the book, and you want to go back and look at it. What are the connections?

Anna Hope, novelist

I remember doing a screenwriting module on my master's degree, and initially thinking, 'Oh my god, dirty plot! It's so cheap.' The writers that I really loved were modernist, so I didn't think I was interested in plot – but it was an incredibly helpful module on story structure, and I still go back to it. It's so interesting, this relationship that I think particularly novelists have with structure. It can feel almost shameful to talk about it.

Rumaan Alam, novelist

It surprises me how certain writers never speak about the reader, and never think about what the book is intended to provide. Yes, every writer has to have a message, whether it's political or aesthetic or spiritual – there's a reason they're creating the fiction they're creating – but their fundamental responsibility is to the reader and her pleasure. Books should be a pleasure.

You can define that very broadly. There are readers who find James Joyce, or Virginia Woolf at her most difficult, to be extraordinarily pleasurable, and then there are readers whose definition of pleasure is Danielle Steel or Barbara Cartland. That's fine; there are multiple ways to be pleased, just as you can prefer chocolate ice cream or vanilla. I think as the writer, though, you have to understand whether your reader wants chocolate or vanilla, and what you're giving her. If she wants vanilla ice cream, and you're serving her the ingredients but not the ice cream itself, then you haven't done your job. A novel has to obey certain rules. If it breaks those rules, it must have a reason for breaking them, and the reason has to be as pleasurable as when they're unbroken.

That revelation has really changed how I think about my work – which is to think about the reader's expectations, and how to toy with them but deliver something to that reader nonetheless. I don't want sentences to accrue when they're not in service of the book. A book is a machine, and the machine has to pull you through.

There is also a real problem of inflation in the contemporary novel. Novels are too long. Ted Hughes talked about this with respect to the typewriter, so it's a conversation that's quite old – that if the technology is guiding the creation then it's very difficult to say, 'Is this right or is it wrong?' Did the typewriter make it too easy to write at length, and did the computer make it too easy to write at still greater length?

I work as a critic a fair amount. I've stopped saying this in my criticism, because at this point it's enough – but most of the books that I see are too long. There are some writers who are much more disposed to economy, and there are occasional, really beautiful long novels that are absolutely astonishing to sink into and just a marvel. But I think that generally, a lot of books could stand to go on a diet.

I wonder whether writers have a feeling that it's not import-ant enough if it's short.

Oh, of course – that's 100 per cent what it is. Then the book is just padded. Coetzee is a good example. *Disgrace* is such a slender book, and it's astonishing. A masterpiece. So tight. Patrick Modiano, one of my favourite living writers – his books are tiny, very tiny. You could read one in an afternoon, and they're bottomless pits. They look like puddles and they turn out to be oceans. The idea that length correlates to significance is so juvenile. It's such an error.

Sathnam Sanghera, journalist, novelist and non-fiction writer

In my late twenties, when I had been working at the *Financial Times* for several years, I got a deal to write a memoir. I found it technically really difficult. The longest thing I'd written at that stage was probably 2,000 words. I remember when I wrote my first column for the *FT*, it was meant to be a weekly column and I was filling in for someone else – but the first one took me three weeks, so it was unsustainable. I'm a slow writer, and it took me ages to learn how to do it – then to go from that to 100,000 words is quite a leap.

My agent and my editor held my hand and helped me. One of the chapters was about having my hair cut for the first time, as a teenager. My first draft of the scene was 800 words; by the time I finished the manuscript, two years later, that chapter was 5,000 words. I wrote something brief, and then I kept on adding and adding descriptions and insights and conversations. That's the advice I would give to someone starting out – get down your first draft, and it doesn't matter if it feels insubstantial. You can always add to it later.

Curtis Sittenfeld, novelist

Often at the beginning of a book I wildly underestimate how many pages it will need and how complicated the plot will be. I said to my editor that I thought *Rodham* would be 120 pages, a novella – and I think it's 416 pages. It was very optimistic of me.

I believe myself to be starting at the beginning, but sometimes it will later turn out that I started on page seventy and I just didn't know it. I start writing, and after ten or twenty pages I create my first outline – I don't think of it as my first outline, but ten outlines later, it turns out that it was. Honestly, the strange thing about *Rodham* is that it was not until I'd been writing it for two years that I recognised what the actual structure would be.

I think in terms of plot, the order of scenes, what happens in each scene, what's shown and what's summarised. I think of it like a dinosaur skeleton in a natural-history museum. Let's say that you uncover dinosaur bones in a field somewhere: how you assemble them is very important, and that's the structure, but the material you put over them doesn't matter that much. The sequence of events, I think, is much more important than the mood or the sentence, and so whether you covered the dinosaur bones with what looks like dinosaur skin or you covered them with a gigantic sheet, they would still retain a lot of the same shape.

Do you think of it in terms of the reader experience – building suspense and having surprising things happen at the right moments?

Well, I don't think to myself, 'I need to create suspense here,' or 'I need to make social commentary.' Let's say the bit of information that emerges in this scene is that this woman realises she forgot her key, or this person's toe is run over by someone's bike. There's the thing that happens, and then there's the most interesting way of depicting it, or having two characters interact. Instinctively, there's probably also a part of me that's thinking, 'Oh, that was a really long but quiet scene, and so my next scene should be short and more exciting,' but I'm not even aware of this thought. What I'm consciously thinking is, 'What should happen next? What should happen next?'

You would think, based on this description, that I write riveting murder mysteries.

You do write riveting books, they're just not necessarily thrillers.

Sometimes people will say to me, 'I find your book to be a page-turner and I don't know why.' I take that as extremely high praise. It's almost like somebody saying, 'Your features aren't that great, yet you're beautiful' – which, by the way, no one has ever said to me. I like to feel as though I'm a magician and the reader doesn't really know what's going on.

I also will say that writing is the thing that I've spent tons and tons of time on for more than thirty-five years. I certainly know not everyone likes my books, which I'm totally at peace with, and there are so many activities where I don't have very good instincts – but I feel that my fiction instincts are very fully formed.

Emily St. John Mandel, novelist and screenwriter

I found the plot of your book The Glass Hotel *continually surprising in a way that I really enjoyed; it wasn't a conventional arc that you would be likely to see in a film version. I think we have a greater tolerance on the page for not being able to sense where we're going. Both formats can be wonderful to consume – but different.*

Perhaps it is just what we've been conditioned to expect from these different media. I think we do have more tolerance for literary fiction, where we're often just following somebody without knowing what's happening. If you're watching a TV show, and it's been five minutes and he's still walking down that street, it's like, where's the action? Is a car going to explode?

Becoming a screenwriter has given me a new appreciation for why adaptations are so different from the source material. It used to be that I would see a TV show or a movie based on a book I loved, and I'd think, 'That is so different from the original.' What screenwriting has made me realise is that it has to be, because the dramatic requirements are completely different.

A good example is my novel *Station Eleven*, which became a TV series. In the novel there's this character Jeevan, who's off on his own wandering through a landscape. In prose, I can show his thoughts and give him a lonely interior life and make it interesting. You can't really do that on TV: it's just a guy walking through a forest in the snow. It's not enough. So in the television adaptation of the story, he has a sidekick, eight-year-old Kirsten. They can talk to each other, so you can get the same ideas across that I could just write out on the page.

Ruben Östlund, film-maker

It's very important for me that each scene should be strong enough to stand by itself. If someone decides to watch just that single fragment of the film, I want them to have an experience. I have always tried to avoid using scenes only to give information for the bigger plot. I want every single scene to be the best scene in the film.

I also want the audience to experience the time that they're sitting in the cinema in a dynamic way, and I know that if I'm watching a movie, as I'm getting closer to the end, the film-maker needs to push in some energy. It's very much about rhythm, I think. If all the scenes have the same rhythm, then you're challenging the audience in a specific way – or you can break the rhythm with a fast-paced scene, and then a slower scene, and then a faster scene again.

Since I'm the director and the editor of my films as well as the writer, I like to have test screenings where I sit with an audience and watch the first edit, which is approximately one hour longer than the final version will be. Sitting with the audience, you realise, 'Ah, here it's going too fast. Here it's going too slow. Here I have to go in later in the scene, or I have to go out earlier.'

I want everything to be unique; I don't want it to be comparable with any other film that I have seen or that the audience have seen. I want to take them on a journey where they are surprised, and there will be turning points that they didn't expect – therefore I have to approach every film in a new way.

Grace Dent, restaurant critic, YA writer and memoirist

Say I'm going to write about a restaurant: I'm umming and ahing about opening a document, and I don't know where I'm going to start the review, but then a really good line will come into my head. Now, years ago, I would have thought, 'I need to fit this line in somewhere. How many paragraphs before I can fit in this great joke?' Now I just think, 'Right, that's the start.' The reader can catch up with me.

If you're writing journalism, say the things you need to say really quickly – that's how you draw people in. Say the difficult thing. Instead of spending 350 words to say, 'Actually, I'm quite livid about this,' start by saying you're livid. If the thing that you hated most in the restaurant was the toilets, start with that. No one's going to look for the best bit of your article, so get in there and do that bit first. Once you've got it, there's a chance that how great it is will jig you along – and before you know it, you'll start to fire out even better things.

Andrew Billen, journalist and interviewer

I'm absolutely in awe of feature writers who can go into the office and just write the piece, holding it all in their head. Simon Hoggart, who was a great writer, used to come into the *Observer* office when I worked there. He'd sit down at twelve o'clock, and it was like automatic writing – by one o'clock the piece would be finished, completely faultless, and off he'd go for a boozy lunch. With my intellect, I need to plan any piece I write, really quite exactly.

I get a transcript of the interview I've done, and I go through it and take note of what was said on each page. I stick that on the window above my desk. Then on the other side of my desk, I have an essay plan that refers to the page numbers of the quotes in the transcript that illustrate the points I'm making.

I think every piece should have an argument, and an end that talks back to the beginning. Occasionally, if the final quote from the interviewee is very good, I'll let it trail off into infinity, like a documentary ending without any sound over the credits – but generally, I like a smart-alec ending. The problem with that is, as we all know, most readers don't get to the end of your piece – so all that effort is usually wasted, I suspect.

Maggie O'Farrell, novelist

Structure is very important to me and I think about it a lot. I have lots of plans of the book I'm writing, which look like flow charts. I'm looking at one right now. It's five different stages of the second part of the novel, and coming off it is this web of different scenes that have to be written. I've crossed off the ones that I've done and I can see the ones that I still need to do.

I make these diagrams based on where I think the book is going to go, but I really like it when the book diverges from my very vague plan. I always feel that will be a good point for the reader. The book has acquired its pulse, and it says, 'Actually, I'm not going from A to B like your diagram says – I'm going from A to C or D.' It takes off on its own momentum.

So you don't resist and try to make it stick to the plan?

Never. I think rules and plans are definitely made to be broken. It's a very good sign, and I always try to work on instinct as much as I can. Having said that, there have been lots of instances where after the first or second draft, I have completely rethought the structure. I have four of the largest pinboards that you can possibly buy, and often on the day of panic, I will suddenly draw lots of flow charts and diagrams and plan it all out.

The novel I wrote with the most complicated structure was *This Must Be the Place*, and I think I used all four pinboards for that. It was very polyphonic – lots of voices, and also lots of chronological strands that were arranged in a non-chronological order. It was a stretch, but I enjoyed it. You think, 'There's too much emphasis on this particular time frame, or this particular character's voice,' and so you need to rethink it. 'Which of these chapters speaks to the others – and if I pull this chapter from the third in line to the seventh, what knock-on effect will it have on the rest of the story?' You have to decide which event gives birth to the next event and how a plot arc knits together – where are the gaps and where are the joins? An interaction between characters might have effects on three or four people involved.

Then if you are trying to write a novel with a thread of mystery to it, you've got to think really carefully. Are there enough signposts for the reader to find their way through? If the reader is told too much, that's also frustrating, because they feel as if you think they're stupid, so it's tricky. The breadcrumb trail needs to be visible but not too obvious. Can my readers trust me here? Can they follow me?

Graham Norton, novelist

I had published two memoirs, and then I met the author David Nicholls at a book event, and I said to him, 'I'm trying to write a novel.' He said, 'Look, give yourself a structure, do a story outline. You don't have to stick to it, but at least you've got scaffolding and you know where you're going.' I did that and it was really useful.

What I found very hard sometimes, though, was just the getting there. I know I'm at A, and I need to get to B, and I think, 'What, is someone going to tell them that? How are they going to find that out?' I just want to get on with the meat of the story, and actually, I can't. There's got to be a bit of fat, there's got to be a bit of bone, there's got to be a bit of packaging. Left to my own devices, I think I would write very short stories.

Kit de Waal, novelist and short-story writer

The first two novels I wrote were never published. When I started working on each of them, I sat down and thought, 'Ooh, let's see where we go with this' – and they were crap. So for *My Name Is Leon* and the novels I've written since, I have used a spreadsheet to really plot out what I want to say and how.

The spreadsheet is a blueprint of how the novel's going to be structured. I wouldn't say it covers every chapter, but it covers chunks of chapters. I knew, for example, that in *Leon* I had to describe his life with Sylvia. I would write on the spreadsheet, 'Leon's life with Sylvia', what that might contain and, most importantly, whether or not I have to seed something in there. For example, Sylvia talking about Maureen all the time drives Leon mad, because it's like she's taking ownership of her, and so I put that in there: 'Don't forget to mention . . .'. Also sprinkled throughout the spreadsheet are little sunshine icons to remind me not to be too intense and depressing. I do have a tendency to write about difficult subjects, and it can be a hard read, so I will write something like, 'This has to be funny' – because otherwise the misery is relentless, and nobody wants to read that.

Do you do that spreadsheet before you start, or is it a work in progress while you write?

I might do scraps of writing at the beginning – a character study or a scene – but basically nine months will be spent on the spreadsheet, and on plotting the writing as opposed to writing the book. The book comes afterwards. I don't look at the spreadsheet much once I've done it, because I know the book by then. To me, the spreadsheet becomes the novel. It's like sketching out an oil painting, and then all you've got to do is fill in the colour.

Meg Mason, novelist

There's a lot of maths in novel writing. My first novel, *You Be Mother*, was set over the course of a year. I was learning on it, so I just blithely started it, and it wasn't until the end of that first draft that the copy editor saw it and said, 'But it's August, and you've said she's wearing a thick cardigan, and she'd be boiling.' I had to go back and retro-engineer all the months and the times, and it was so complicated and so much work that when I sat down to write my next novel, I made a spreadsheet with everybody's date of birth and an enormous mega-chart for the wall, with the years of the entire novel down the left-hand side, and what happened when and what season, so that I couldn't ever get tangled up.

Mhairi McFarlane, novelist

What would you say are the essential beats of a romantic comedy?
    You need obstacles, obviously, and you also need a time pressure. If your romantic leads can get together at their own leisure any time in the next five years, because they live around the corner from each other, it's fundamentally less exciting than if one of them is going to go away. I will shamelessly point out that Sally Rooney's *Normal People*, which is classed as literary fiction, follows loads of the rules: there are implausible misunderstandings; there's the fact that one of them is going to go away, and all the rest of it. An awful lot of romances have these things underneath

them, and when you watch or read them, they're so satisfying partly because they've observed these rules. We don't know why it works, but it just does.

In your books there's always a secondary cast of friends who have their own concerns in the world, and often their own subplots.

Yes, and I think one of the toughest challenges I've found is, how do you put other stories into your novel and service them properly? Because it's very frustrating when you feel you've invested in something early on and it doesn't pay off later – but at the same time, you'd never want people to be skipping that chapter to get to the next thing, and so you really don't want to take them out of the A-plot for too long. In terms of the sweet spot for subplots and secondary characters, I think you have to use instinct, but be quite stingy. You have to make everybody absolutely earn their time. If they're going to walk into a room, they'd better earn being in that room.

George Saunders, short-story writer

I'm going to make a case for causality, in the same way that if I were talking to a bunch of dancers, I would make a case for gravity: it's just what we have to work against. If I say to you, 'Hey, I've got this incredible story I have to tell you – it's only eight pages,' I think you're automatically going to expect causation. You want A to cause B to cause C, and when you really look at great stories, that's where the meaning gets made. Scrooge is stingy. We expect from the beginning that he's going to get unstingy. How does that happen? That's where the story's message lies, in the causality.

Once you know what the form of the short story does best, you've signed up for certain responsibilities. If I say to you, 'Once upon a time, a guy was really happy, and then the next day he was just as happy, and the third day, he woke up and he was the same level of happy that he had been before' – I mean, you understand that this is not a story. You want the happiness to cause something. It's not a rule but it's a law, and even in *Waiting for Godot*, where nothing's causing anything, we feel the weight of the causality. The play is brilliant because it resists it, but that doesn't mean it denies its existence.

It's kind of Hollywood stuff: a woman sees her old boyfriend in a store. If it doesn't cause anything, that's an anecdote. But if she sees her old boyfriend in a store, goes out to the car, and the baby starts crying and she begins to doubt her marriage, then suddenly we've got some causation going on, and the story starts to narrow its focus.

You have also talked about the idea that a story needs to escalate. Is it the A-causing-B-causing-C that gives you the sense of escalation?

I think so, and all these things are related. If I say, 'God, Hattie, you're not going to believe what happened this morning,' well, that's a pretty good start to a story, and it's implied that something exciting has happened that's meaningful. If it isn't exciting and it isn't meaningful – if it doesn't have causation and escalation – you're going to feel a little let down. 'Why did he tell me that? That's not interesting.'

James Acaster, stand-up comic and author

So much of stand-up is that it has to suit you as a comedian, so there's no definitive good structure for a set. For me, having a persona who overanalyses tiny things in life meant that it made sense for the structure of the show to be a little bit more considered. My onstage persona wouldn't just do an hour of jokes without a structure and then leave.

My first two shows didn't have an arc – they were just a series of routines, and I was learning. Then my third show had two halves. The first half of it was short jokes that were not connected to each other, and the second half was this theme of trying to clear the name of Yoko Ono, but it had callbacks to all of the short jokes from earlier.

I think callbacks are really interesting. They crop up in lots of different kinds of writing and entertainment, and even in journalism. Often what journalists will do in a feature is to plant some sort of idea near the beginning, and then call back to it in the final paragraph to wrap things up. Obviously, in comedy it's something that can build layers of laughter as you go through a show.

There are really lazy ways of doing a callback that I've definitely done in the past, where you literally repeat the thing that you said earlier, and not for any particular reason. You're repeating it in the same context and under the same lens, and it's just showing people the same thing again. That can get a laugh just because their head tells them, 'That's familiar – laugh at it.' But it's empty and not that nourishing, and they go away with the illusion of structure, as the comic Stewart Lee has said.

I think a good callback presents the same thing in a different light. When you have to write a show in a year, to do it at the next Edinburgh Festival, you naturally write material that links up and has a lot of running themes, because that's where you are in your life. Natural opportunities for callbacks present themselves all the time, especially if you're trying out these routines in twenty-minute sets, and you're going onstage every night and trying to find links between them.

When you then build them into an hour-long show, you have opportunities for callbacks that aren't as obvious: 'The link between this routine and this routine is actually this emotional thing.' That can later become a callback, when those routines are now quite far apart over the course of an hour. The audience don't see it coming, because you're only talking about how emotionally it's the same. That's more surprising and more fun for them, I think.

But it has to make sense; it has to be figure-outable. It's like a good M. Night Shyamalan film – and, by the way, there is only one. The twist at the end makes you think, 'How did I not see that?' He's been showing it to you the whole film. But then his other films, where the twists aren't as good, make you feel, 'How could I have possibly known that? It relies on a bit of information that none of us knew, so it's not satisfying.'

It's the same with callbacks in comedy. If it's too easy to figure out, it's bad, but if you try to hide it from them too much, it doesn't make sense. It has to be something where the logic is inbuilt – it's all there, and you could've figured it out if you wanted to, but you didn't because you got swept up in the show. Then the callback brings you back to that place, and it feels exciting and fun.

André Aciman, novelist, memoirist and essayist

My first editor told me one thing that was very useful: that if I want to do something in the middle of the book, I need to have prepared the reader far earlier, without the reader's awareness, for that moment to really blossom. You plant the seed early, and later you reap whatever it is you planted – and you get a kind of Wagnerian effect, where the little melody that you started with becomes far more complex. Always write with an eye forward and backwards.

Elif Shafak, novelist

Sometimes intellectuals, authors or poets seem to forget that there are different ways of storytelling. I have a lot of respect for the tradition of the Western novel. I love it, I cherish it, I treasure it. I'm also aware that there is a more cyclical or circular way of storytelling, which is mostly found in oral culture. I grew up with those stories, and someone coming from a Chinese, Middle Eastern, South American or African background may be very familiar with other traditions of oral culture and other types of storytelling. There isn't a single way of writing a novel, and we can't be Eurocentric in our expectations of what it should be like – I find that thinking very dangerous. We have to open our horizons, and that requires reading extensively from different cultural backgrounds, and I'm not sure we're doing that enough.

John Rentoul, journalist

I remember early in my career on the *Independent* being asked to do a 600-word background feature on some aspect of the Labour Party, which they needed by five o'clock. This was at three o'clock. I was absolutely terrified – but I did know the subject, so I didn't have to make many calls, and I just wrote it. After that I lost my fear of short deadlines.

I get those newspaper assignments too sometimes, and I love it. I go into a very specific frame of mind: I have to immediately focus.

Exactly. When I'm writing a column, I start with the headline, then think about the subhead, and then the first sentence – and I've got to have a clear idea of where the end is going to be. I don't worry about the middle so much. That takes care of itself.

In terms of the headline, are you thinking, 'What is the strongest thing I want to say about this topic?'

Yes, I'm thinking in terms of clickbait.

Really?

There's nothing wrong with clickbait. I'm thinking, 'What will make people want to read what I've got to say? How can I express it in the most interesting way?' And then you want a first sentence that isn't necessarily summing it all up – but it draws the reader in.

Do you ever worry that in British journalism, the form is dictating the content and tone of conversations about politics? You said you're often thinking in terms of the clickbait headline that's going to draw people in – doesn't that mean that the opinions get more and more extreme?

Yes, but that's always been a problem of journalism. If you think about the criticisms of tabloid journalism in the 1980s, it was that the newspapers simplified and exaggerated, and that there was a coarsening of the public discourse. It's something I'm always struggling with, because I like to think of myself as a more reflective commentator who's often trying to see both sides, or trying to take a contrary position that isn't particularly vivid. But no, I don't think British journalism is any worse than it was. I think it's better than American journalism, which is ghastly. Even the *New York Times* long read, which starts with a long description of the weather and the time of day, and blah, blah, blah . . . You don't get that in British journalism, which is so much more direct. Some long-form American journalism is brilliant, but a lot of it is just too long.

David Nicholls, novelist and screenwriter

With the TV adaptation of Patrick Melrose, *the series of novels by Edward St Aubyn, you boiled down five books to five episodes. Just structurally, where do you begin to approach something like that?*

I've learnt this from experience: the important thing is not to precis the story. If you squeeze everything in but don't give it the time it needs, then yes, people who love the novel will be able to sit there and tick off the bits they like, but it won't work. It will feel like a synopsis rather than a drama in itself. If you're going to make cuts, I always compare it to surgery – you've got to be bold. You've got to say, 'It's better to play this scene at some length and make it land, rather than include everything from the novel and just skitter over it.'

It wasn't actually as big a problem with *Patrick Melrose* as you'd think, because three of the five novels take place in a single setting, over quite a short period of time, and that's easier to adapt than something that leaps across generations. The fourth book, *Mother's Milk*, takes place over four years and with children growing up, which is always a nightmare in an adaptation, so there are much bolder cuts in that. But the first three – *Never Mind*, *Bad News* and *Some Hope* – are pretty faithful, and if things are taken out, it's usually because of repetition.

In the novel of *Bad News*, there's a scene where Patrick goes to a nightclub and tries to pick up this girl and treats her very badly. It's very powerful and uncomfortable and unpleasant in the book, and a very fine piece of writing, and on screen it could have been great – you could have had this 1980s New York nightclub, which would've looked brilliant. But it was repeating a feeling that we'd had in the previous scene, where he'd gone out for dinner with a woman and behaved badly—

So we already had that information about Patrick.

We've had that. You're more forgiving of repetition in a novel than you are on screen. There were drafts of the script where that exists, but it was quite an easy cut.

Robert Popper, screenwriter

My first real comedy job was working for Peter Richardson at *The Comic Strip Presents*. He used to say, 'Don't worry about the funny – just make sure the story is right.'

Later, when I came to make the sitcom *Friday Night Dinner*, that was how I approached it. What is the story? If nothing happens and one thing doesn't lead to another thing, people will turn over.

Then when I was in the writers' room on *South Park*, somebody told me that in a script, you should be able to link the scenes not just with 'and then . . . and then . . .', but with 'therefore . . .' or 'but . . .'. So *because* of what happened in the last scene, something else will happen in the next one. The scenes that don't do that are often the ones I end up cutting. I remember a very funny scene in *Friday Night Dinner* with Paul Ritter as Martin telling a story about his 'best ever' holiday – he went on a caravan holiday with his uncle, which ended with a donkey biting off his uncle's fingers and them spending the rest of the trip at the hospital. Paul did it brilliantly.

We watched it back for the first time, and we all laughed – it was really funny. But the scene didn't move the story on, and we didn't have the time. So we snipped it out straight away. That advice taught me to be ruthless.

6

What can language do?

'My grandmother said to me,
"Swearing isn't big and it isn't clever."
Now I want to say to her, "Yes it is.
My whole career has been built on it."'

GEORGIA PRITCHETT, screenwriter

We make fun of my dad liberally: for being hopeless with technology; for having attempted, in the 1960s, to woo my mum with a curry ready-meal; for wearing moth-eaten jumpers. There are a couple of areas, though, where all mockery falls silent and I can only be proud. I've never met anyone with better social skills than my dad, or anyone who could write a more elegant sentence.

I'll start with the first, because I think it helps to explain the second. My dad goes out of his way to be courteous. He's never obsequious, but he does the simple things that make others feel important: letting strangers go ahead of him; writing thank-you letters. He's also very funny. At our parties, he makes guests laugh, listens to stories, pours drinks. At other people's parties, we wait wearily at the door while he circles the room saying long good-byes. He gets cross if we try to hurry this along. Growing up and learning how to treat people, then, I tried to absorb the practical wisdom and thoughtfulness of my mother and the generous charm of my father.

I get teased by friends from overseas who find British politeness ridiculous. I've dated Europeans and been shocked by their bluntness – until it dawned on me that we are the weird ones, with our careful rituals that can tip into passive aggression. We say, 'Yes, we *could* go there,' instead of 'No, I hate that place,' or 'Maybe I'm remembering it wrong,' instead of 'Your version of events is a barefaced lie,' and we expect our meaning to be understood. Perhaps we take it too far, but I like the underlying principle of respect, and of making little efforts to cushion others from discomfort.

This is how my dad taught me to see the world, but it's also how he taught me to see my job. He's an academic and when I'm grappling with work, he tells me, 'Easy writing makes hard reading.'* What he means is that being painstaking with our raw materials – words, clauses, sentences and paragraphs – is a service. As former *New Yorker* copy editor Mary Norris argues in this chapter, when we break rules of grammar or spelling, we should do so not by accident but thoughtfully, and for some particular effect; the writer must always take care of the reader. My dad is probably the reason why I believe that this is not just about style or communication, but also good manners.

Poets are the experts in being inventive and playful with words, and so they're often asked about language – but I think we sometimes forget that screenwriters, journalists and novelists think hard about it too. What's the funniest word to express this? Should I

---

* Apparently the Irish poet Richard Brinsley Sheridan was the first to coin a version of this. In 'Clio's Protest or, the Picture Varnished', composed in 1771, he wrote: 'You write with ease, to shew your breeding; But easy writing's vile hard reading.'

cut half this sentence, and would it feel more impactful? Could this phrase suggest two things, and would the reader understand that I mean both of them?

It's worth the effort, because as keen readers know, prose has the power to devastate or exhilarate. For me, reading certain writers – not only those in this book, but also Kazuo Ishiguro, or Claire Keegan, or Chimamanda Ngozi Adichie – is similar to watching a prima ballerina or listening to a skilled musician. There's a total mastery of the medium on display, and it's dazzling: the writer seems light as air, able to touch three emotions in ten words and make each resonate. The craft of this is done not on stage, but in the privacy of the computer screen or page, and so I've tried to bring some of it to light in this chapter.

Of course, there are limits to what words can express, as anyone who has been on the periphery of a tragedy will know. Sometimes language is not enough for the experience of being human – or it's far too much: crass and sentimental. The poet Michael Rosen knows something about this. How could he possibly express his anguish after his son's death? He explains in this chapter how he learnt to use the plainest of words and let the reader fill in the rest. We can't always articulate the depths of a feeling – but sometimes, by building language around its outlines, we can help the reader to sense it in the void.

By the way, despite his holey jumpers, my dad is not just popular but exceptionally loved. My mother, sister and I are used to being cornered by friends, family and people we barely know, who express in their own ways how funny he is, how kind, and what he means to them. It doesn't come close to what he means to us, but for that, I don't have the words.

Will Harris, poet and essayist

Poetry feels rebellious. It's a perverse form of communication. It's very short, but it often doesn't make sense, and it forces you to sit with it and weigh up each word.

Ludwig Wittgenstein said, 'Do not forget that a poem, although it is composed in the language of information, is not used in the language-game of giving information.' So a poem uses the same words that we use day to day, but it doesn't play the game of 'Pass me the butter,' or 'Here's what's happening in the news.' I think that's the thing I always liked about it; that's the perverse streak that runs through poetry. It uses words you understand in ways that you don't normally understand them.

Rumaan Alam, novelist

In the opening chapters of your novel Leave the World Behind, *before it becomes clear that something very sinister is happening, you spend time establishing the atmosphere of a family holiday in a way that's unrushed and tantalising. How did you go about building that atmosphere?*

It's a seduction. It's meant to fool the reader. I hope you think, 'Oh, this is a book about an unhappy marriage, or a secret, or a family unravelling or coming together over the course of a holiday' – because that's the convention of literature, and so you recognise it. But even though the pacing of those early chapters is languid and lush, there's also a lot of menace, and it goes back to the only tool that any writer has to work with, which is language.

The language is provocative and the observation is menacing. There's a piece of a Band-Aid wrapper in the car because 'Kids were always needing a Band-Aid, pink skin splitting like summer fruit.' Amanda goes shopping and everything she buys is organic food that's wrapped up in plastic. I could have said that the windows of the car were tinted like a presidential limousine, or like a starlet's sunglasses, or like a certain kind of crystal ashtray popular in the 1970s – but I said they were tinted to keep cancer at bay. That establishes something in the mind of the reader, I think, that you may or may not be fully conscious of.

Kit de Waal, novelist and short-story writer

Dialogue I can do over and over again – I could write a whole book of it. I'm quite good on plotting too, but if someone says to me, 'What colour is Sylvia's hair?', I wouldn't know. I really have to work at that. When I do the first draft of something, I will never describe a room, a day, the weather, what someone looks like or what they're wearing – I cannot do it the first time I write. Then when I go back, on second and subsequent drafts, I texturise it with colour and weather and cold and heat, and make everything more sensual. That's work for me. That's not natural at all.

I was helped by something Philip Pullman said: 'Where does the light come in?' It made a massive difference to me. It can be a figurative question: what are we concentrating on in this scene? But it's also helpful in a literal sense. How does the light fall on the furniture? Is there a window? Is it a candle? Is it a naked bulb? It's a great place to start if you are struggling to describe somewhere.

Jon Ronson, storyteller and author

My writing has always been about what I learnt from people like Kurt Vonnegut and Raymond Carver: to take as complicated an idea as possible and reduce it to something simple and fun to read, where the complicated idea is expressed in the fewest possible words. When you stop overexplaining, you're allowing the reader to read between the lines. It becomes like a partnership between the reader and the writer.

Someone complimented me the other day on a line in my book *Them*. It was about how extremists think of people like me, liberal Jews, as having a fanatical, depraved belief system. I wrote, 'I like it when they say that, because it makes me feel as if I have a belief system.' That's a good example.

Lucy Prebble, playwright and screenwriter

I think there's a general confusion about writing for screen or stage: dialogue is a tiny part of it. Well, maybe that's less true for stage – in Shakespeare's time, you'd say you were going to hear a play, not see a play, and there's a reason for that – but the work of writing is so much more about the story, the turns, what happens and how the characters respond to it. The dialogue is icing, I think. Nice icing, but not the main bulk of the thing.

I recently saw a new production of my first play, *The Sugar Syndrome*. What I saw was a lot of showing off in the dialogue. There was a lot of stuff that people wouldn't say to each other in real life, or – everyone knows what this is – where I was trying to tell the audience something through what the character's saying. That's a really common flaw, and a young writer's flaw, I think.

You're wanting to go, 'Look how clever I am!', or if we're being super kind, you're trying to connect with people, but it's clumsy. Audiences pull back from that because they sense it immediately. They think, 'Well, hang on, I'm not here for you to tell me things that you know.'

Of course, they are. The joke is that you just get better at hiding it. You get better at manipulating them through other means, and all that's really clumsy about having characters say things in order to show the audience what you think is how obvious you're being about it. If you make your feelings and experiences inherent in the movement of the story, your choice of tone, your choice of genre – that will do a lot of the work, and you won't have to overwrite and point things out in dialogue.

That's what screen has taught me, because when you can get really close to the face of an actor, you realise how much more elegant it is to let them do some of the work. I had to learn to stop trying to do other people's jobs for them, which is partly what you're doing when you overwrite – you're not trusting a director or an actor or an audience to understand something, so you're putting it there in print. The audience can sense that lack of trust, and obviously so can actors.

John Mulaney, the stand-up, talks about a moment when he changed his style, which was very wordy. Somebody said to him after a gig, 'You're funny – but these people have no time for your cleverness.' It's a line that always stuck with me, because it was a reminder that one of the things I was trying to do with my writing was to inform and entertain people, and share the excitement about interesting things that I'd discovered. Now when I write, I think really hard: 'What would this be if it wasn't clever?'

So much of my work has been referred to with that word, and

it's actually not a very praising word. It's either 'clever-clever', where you're dismissive of somebody being tricksy, or 'clever clogs', which is someone showing off, or it's an insult to a comedian – if you say, 'Your jokes are clever,' it's really fucking insulting, because it means they're not funny. It's not a word that we use much in praise, and I was always very aware that it was attached to my work. I feel like there's more to me than that, or at least I wanted there to be, and so I started to try to avoid it.

Andrew Billen, journalist and interviewer

A friend once told me that his mother never understood a word I wrote in the *Observer*. I thought, 'Yeah, you're probably right. Why say "the iconography of stardom" in a piece? Why not say the "signs and trappings" instead?' I'm less of an intellectual snob now.

Mona Arshi, poet, novelist and essayist

I love that you work with a dictionary next to you.

It's an incredible toolbox and also essential for writing prompts. We don't have much as poets; we work in short, condensed lines in which we have to say something quickly, and our tools are language, lineation and form. Often an interesting image is made through a counterpoint: two words alongside each other that resonate or generate a spark together like a flint – they ignite.

Is the sensory quality of a word a big part of your thinking?

Yes, your ear is a diagnostic tool that tells you whether or not you've got a good line. The ear is a real bullshit detector, actually. You're not just trying to say something – you also have to make it sound beautiful or interesting. You're communicating through the language of the language, but you're also communicating through the music of the language, and sometimes they're doing opposite things.

Emily St. John Mandel, novelist and screenwriter

Rhythm is very important to me, I think in the same way that it is for poets. I read the work aloud during the revision process, which kills my voice because it's sometimes hundreds of pages – but that's the way I catch awkward sentences that I might otherwise have missed, or hear when the rhythm is off and needs to be revised.

What I'm trying to do is write prose that's lucid and clear but also beautiful. When I was in my early twenties I read a lot of Nabokov, and his prose is so beautiful but it's really ornate in a way that can feel fussy. I think I tried to emulate that with my first novel, which is a trap a lot of novelists fall into. You catch on that you have some talent for this thing you're trying to do, and what can take over is a goal of, 'Let's try to make this sentence as pretty and fancy as possible.'

After my first novel, I read a lot of detective fiction, and I read *The Executioner's Song* by Norman Mailer, which has the sparest prose. It really changed my style, and since then, I've been going for clarity. Can you find the beauty in an impeccably clear sentence and paragraph and page? That's what I'm always striving for.

Maggie O'Farrell, novelist

When you're writing, your brain is firing on many different levels all at once. You've got to be thinking about the actual story, but also the dialogue – does it sound natural? Would this character actually speak like that? You're also considering the tense or the case and the grammar. Then if you use a metaphor, you have to ask yourself, does it seem at all familiar or clichéd? Does it sound startling – or is it too interesting, too distracting?

Later, you might have to cut out some of your most beloved phrases. You should be asking yourself, 'Why do I love it? Is it too much?'

James Acaster, stand-up comic and author

I was always OK at creating the structure of a joke or routine, but choosing the right words was something that I hadn't really paid any attention to until seeing Mike Wozniak doing comedy. I listened to him and thought, 'If he changed that word to something else, this routine wouldn't work.'

That is a big part of the comedy tool-belt – to choose the right words each time. Half the time, the funny idea you've got in your head *is* funny, but you're not communicating it to the audience because you're using bog-standard language, or language that's a bit too vague. You're hoping that they see what's funny about it the same way that you do – whereas if you choose the exact right word, they can't help but visualise the same thing that you're visualising. Then it works every night. That was a huge lesson early on: if you want to stop the audience staring at you while you waffle on, nail down your language.

I had a routine in my third show about the spoons at the restaurant Wahaca. People steal their spoons, because they're really nice, but Wahaca have a policy that if you bring the stolen spoons back in January, they'll give you free tacos. I think the line I had was,

'It's a double-win for Wahaca, because they get their spoons back, and they get to watch the thief eat tacos that I imagine have been interfered with beyond belief.'

'Interfered with' was funnier than saying 'spat in', and 'beyond belief' was just a funny phrase at the end. That routine wouldn't have been funny phrased differently, because I think before you get to the punchline, the audience can guess what it is, or at least they're halfway there. There's a lot of set-up, because you've got to explain the whole scheme at Wahaca, and when you say you return the spoons and they give you free tacos, the audience are already thinking, 'I wouldn't want to eat those tacos . . .'. You still need to surprise them with the punchline. Sometimes even if they're ahead of you, you can articulate it better and funnier than they have, and you can surprise them.

Graham Norton, novelist

It's only when I'm revising my drafts of a novel that I realise: 'Wow, I have had so many people leaning on things,' you know. 'Oh god, how did this happen? How did I use that word so many times?' Then you have to go in and hack away. In one book, nobody leans. In the next book – Jesus, it's non-stop.

Meg Mason, novelist

Stuck on my wall, there's a funny line from a Victoria Wood stand-up routine. It's about when you're a teenager and you have a boyfriend who you think is an absolute lothario, until he comes home and meets your parents for the first time. Then you see him through your parents' eyes, and he's the most desperate little weed. The line is just the mother saying, 'Did I not offer you a fork, Clint?'

Everything I ever want to do as a writer is in that line, and her phrasing and her choice of name. There's a tiny bit of passive aggression in there. You know that she has already offered him a fork, that he's eating horribly. In eight words, she relates this entire scene and all of the humour and pathos of it. I have it on my wall as a permanent reminder: if you need more than eight words to do it, that's too many.

When I read *Grief Is the Thing with Feathers* by Max Porter, which I absolutely love, I remember being amazed and discombobulated by the language. I just couldn't understand: where did he get it from? How did he create this, and how did he know to make the characters talk like that? Then I heard Max Porter speaking at the Sydney Writers' Festival, and that's just how he talks, essentially. It's his own energy and his own voice.

It helped me set a rule never to use the thesaurus. I decided that if I didn't know the word, I didn't need the word, and to trust myself that I didn't need to try to sound smarter than I am. That has really helped.

Your own voice is the one thing that you have that no one else has. Don't try to write to sound like someone else, or even a better version of yourself. If you write as your real, daily self, you can sustain it, because it's organically you. It will be unique and there will always be more where it came from.

David Sedaris, essayist and performer

When I read the novel *No One Is Talking About This* by Patricia Lockwood, I had to turn down every single page and underline things, because it was like she invented language. I often feel that way reading Lorrie Moore's work too. I'm not in any way poetic. I don't have that mind, and I really admire people who do have it. The best I can do is write as cleanly as possible, and try not to draw attention to the writing – because if you don't have that skill, and you try to draw attention to it, it is excruciating.

I do care a lot about the rhythm, and so it's great to go on tour and read things out loud. I mean, try to read Raymond Carver out loud: you have to stitch the sentences together, because every one has the same number of syllables in it, and it just lays there. He was a huge inspiration to me when I first started writing, but I don't enjoy his work any more.

Georgia Pritchett, screenwriter

Some of the shows you've worked on – The Thick of It, Veep, Succession – *are known for their clever dialogue and, in particular, some very funny and profane one-line insults. What is the craft of those?*

I remember thinking very primly when I was asked to work on *The Thick of It*, 'Well, I don't think I know enough swear words.' Then Armando Iannucci asked me to write a diatribe for the character of Malcolm Tucker, and it all came pouring out of me, this torrent of filth – it was astonishing.

People sometimes say that swearing is lazy; we were trying to make it the opposite of that. We tried to be very imaginative and creative, and make the description more interesting by employing some unexpected and unusual words. The sensibility, if you can use that word about swearing, was rather baroque and elegant and creative and flowery – not just people saying 'fuck you' to each other. That's the real difference, and I think it was a big shock. When *Veep* first appeared in the States, it was unlike anything they'd seen, and the difference was not really using swearing as an aggressive insult, but using it as a sort of descriptive tool.

My grandmother said to me, 'Swearing isn't big and it isn't clever.' Now I want to say to her, 'Yes, it is. My whole career has been built on it.'

John Rentoul, journalist

I used to poke fun on Twitter at the use of clichés, and people seemed to like it, and eventually I turned it into a book, *The Banned List*. It all started with someone saying, 'It's the economy, stupid' on a BBC TV report. That was a catchphrase from Bill Clinton's 1992 election campaign and it's dying out now, but at the time everybody used it in political commentary. It just meant, 'The economy is quite important.' You would see it in political articles or hear it in TV broadcasts when the person couldn't think of anything more original to say.

Is it the laziness of a cliché that bothers you?

Yes. When it crashes into your brain, you think, 'Well, I've only got a limited amount of time here. Don't tell me something I've heard a million times before, which adds nothing to my understanding of the issue.' It just tells you that the speaker doesn't know anything.

So it's the emptiness of the words, the lack of information.

I suppose it's to do with my impatience and intolerance, really.

I don't know about that. If the purpose of language is to understand each other though, a cliché can be a shortcut.

Yes, I accept that. There's that dreadful line in George Orwell's essay 'Politics and the English Language' about never using a 'figure of speech which you are used to seeing in print'. I mean, that's an absolutely impossible test. If you used only original phrases all the time then people wouldn't follow what you were saying, because they'd have to stop and decode it all – but it's obviously better to be at that end of the spectrum than just trotting out one cliché after another. If the figure of speech is not adding anything, or if there's a plainer way of putting it, then I'd prefer that. I prefer my language to be full of meaning and denser, rather than being padded out.

What are the specific ways that a journalist works with language?

Most journalists are trying to report information as clearly and as quickly as they can, so they don't really have time to worry about style, which is why a lot of clichés come in, I suppose. The journalist I admire most is Alastair Campbell, who became Prime Minister Tony Blair's press secretary and spokesman. It was his economy of expression, directness, use of plain language – he was brilliant and also quick, and it's difficult to be both of those things together. Speed usually leads to clumsy language. One of the reasons Blair hired him was because he worked for a tabloid newspaper, the *Mirror*, so he was used to short, clear sentences and direct communication, but those are virtues in any writing, in my view.

I write a weekly column for the *Independent*, 'Mea Culpa', which looks at clichés, malapropisms and grammar errors that have slipped into the newspaper. I love doing it, although I always feel nervous about criticising my colleagues, especially the younger journalists, so I never name the writer who has made a mistake. It's difficult to be a cheerful curmudgeon, but I try to do it with a light touch, and I constantly make the point that there isn't a right and wrong – it's just a question of knowing what readers expect. You should know what the conventions are in order to avoid irritating people. Obviously, you want to do better than that – you want to actually engage and interest the reader, but the starting point is to avoid annoying them.

Do you really believe there's no right or wrong, or are you being tactful?

No, I really do. Language is what people use, and so if they say, 'I was sat at the table,' – and they do – then that's not wrong. I would say, 'I was sitting at the table,' because that's the older usage, and I think the newer usage puts some people off. It's a constant debate, and you've got to respect how people use language. 'Mea Culpa' is always about how we can sharpen the *Independent*'s communication with its readers.

Untangling ugly syntax is often a problem, and so I enjoy giving examples of where sentences go particularly wrong. Sometimes a writer ends up saying the opposite of what they mean: that a threat 'cannot be underestimated', or something like that, and you can see how that happens, and it happens quite a lot. I try to be helpful by pointing these things out and hoping that people learn from it.

Then I've got several running campaigns. For example, I don't like the words 'ongoing' or 'upcoming'. 'Ongoing' is almost always unnecessary. We had it during COVID-19, with journalists referring to the 'ongoing pandemic'. I mean, we're a newspaper – which pandemic do you think we're talking about? Sometimes there are special cases where people want to talk about something that has started happening and is still happening, in which case you say 'continuing' – because that's normal English.

You don't think 'ongoing' is normal English?

No. It's horrible. It's jargon. It sounds like it came out of a business seminar.

And what's wrong with 'upcoming'?

'Forthcoming' is what we mean – something that's going to be happening soon. 'Upcoming' is a recent invention. Of course, these are actually matters of taste – you can't even say there are rules and conventions. I just don't like the newer forms.

I tried to campaign for 'for ever' as two words, but I'm afraid I've lost that one. I think if you use 'forever' as an adjective, as in a 'forever relationship', then obviously that's a single word, but otherwise, I like it separate. I campaign against 'amid' all the time, because journalists love using 'amid', and that really is lazy. It's just a way of cramming stuff together in a sentence: 'Eight Labour frontbenchers resigned amid a row about Gaza.' I mean, get rid!

What should it be instead?

Whatever the appropriate English word is – in that context, 'because of'.

The 'Mea Culpa' column mostly comes from readers who write in because they've spotted errors. Do they ever catch you out?

Yes, some of my regular correspondents occasionally say, 'If I may take issue with your column this week, I think you meant . . .' and they're usually right. It's usually something I've written in a hurry, and I haven't thought it through.

Jesse Armstrong, screenwriter

I spend a lot of time thinking about language when I'm writing. I think all prose writers know they will get better by reading more – but I'm not sure screenwriters realise that the same principle applies to them. There's no real way of learning, other than listening, watching and reading a lot.

There are similarities between comedy and poetry in terms of the precision and concision of word choice necessary to make it work. There's also a shared allusiveness there, I think; a really good line of comedy or poetry almost says more than you can literally express. Some people have a great ear, and vernacular speech is immediately available to them – but a lot of us need to work at getting that brevity, allusiveness and precision. In a screenplay, the dialogue doesn't have to sound like people you hear when you're walking around; it can be stylised, but it does need to have a relationship to reality.

This is a terrifying thing to say, and it's why the job is potentially endless: you can have an almost infinite ambition for every single line. You probably shouldn't think about that when you're first writing a scene, because it could be paralysing, but when you come back to the script, you should be aware that each line can be expressive of character, it can move plot forward, it can be a true example of either comedy or pathos, and it can be a thought about how the world is. It's very possible to fit all of that into three or four words. You need to have a lot of ambition and respect for your audience: every line really counts, so pack it full of everything that it can be.

At the same time, remember that it has to come out of that character's mouth very precisely, and you should also constantly be thinking, 'Or maybe we should cut this line, and it should just be a look from the actor.' You're working and working to express something, but it's an actor who's going to perform it, and the audience may enjoy it not being said out loud. Do all of your work, but still be aware that however much you love the voice you're giving to the characters, it might not be what the audience need at this moment.

Elif Shafak, novelist

You have written some books in Turkish and others in English. Does it feel the same to write in both languages, or do you feel that you're putting on slightly different identities?

It's not the same, to be honest. I'm an immigrant; my connection with the English language is quite different than that with the Turkish language. Turkish is my mother tongue, the language of my grandmother, and my connection with it is quite emotional – whereas with English, it's more cerebral and intellectual, which I also need.

It was a risk for me to write in a language that was not native to me, and I think that as immigrants we know there will always be a gap between our minds and our tongues. The mind runs faster than the tongue, and you're always trying to catch up, but that's quite intimidating and quite frustrating. Yet something tells me to keep going. Maybe it's the need for a sense of freedom. That's what it is for me, writing in English. I feel lighter, and I need that sense of lightness. Being a Turkish writer is very heavy – the words are heavy. Somehow, writing in English gave me a sense of freedom but also cognitive flexibility. It's like you take a step back and paradoxically, you're able to take a closer look at the culture you come from.

That said, I think what I like most is the commute between languages. Turkish and English are completely different in grammar and vocabulary. To this day, if my writing has melancholy, sorrow and longing, I find these things much easier to express in Turkish – but when it comes to humour, irony and satire, I find them much easier in English.

Meg Wolitzer, novelist

In recent years I've had the chance to hear actors read my work aloud. When writers read aloud, sometimes we rush through to get to the end, or maybe that's just me – but actors slow down, and when they linger, you really hear the language. You know, it would be really nice to have an actor come to your house and read your output every day, and then just leave. If they're between shows, everybody wins.

I will spend so long on a line or paragraph because I need it to convey the way it feels inside me. I don't want it to be a dead sentence, just walking people across a room. Not every sentence should be the best thing in a book, but you want it all to have an aliveness to it, and you want it all to be as close as possible to the emotional experience you're trying to convey. Sometimes the access that a writer has is amazing: how did they make that beautiful leap from this kitchen to somewhere far away, and it makes absolute sense? Language really thrills me.

Have you ever come up against the limits of what language can express?

Yes. If characters have been through something enormous,

what are you going to say? Do you end the scene or chapter in a way that seems cryptic, but is actually hiding the fact that you really didn't know? I don't like that – I'm always uneasy when I find it. I go back to 'What is it like?' Rather than making grand statements, just showing what an experience is like can be a kind of balm.

When you're describing intense emotional states, is there an interplay between trying to express it, but also trying to hold back?

Oh, absolutely. A line break is also a powerful moment – to know when to stop, to imagine what was said. Line breaks can be like rests in music. The conversation that the reader and the book have is private and intense. I don't want to be this intrusive person telling you exactly how to feel, so sometimes I go back and I just take it out. If you're lingering on a vibrating note, that can be much more powerful.

Michael Rosen, poet and author

Your son Eddie died in 1999, and you didn't write for over a year. What do you remember about how it felt not to be able to write, and what it felt like when you came back to writing?

It felt like a sort of blank – that there weren't any words that could express what I felt. Words weren't satisfactory. They couldn't come up to it. The feelings were so raw and profound that if I put down on the page, 'I feel sad,' I had this sense of the inadequacy of language.

The big thing that broke the dam was reading Raymond Carver's poem 'Locking Yourself Out, Then Trying to Get Back In'. It uses very plain language. Americans are so good at expressing the deepest things in very ordinary words – they don't feel it necessary to write great convoluted sentences. You can talk onto the page with a certain dryness, and you don't have to be overly demonstrative.

In the poem, he's locked himself out – you know, an everyday occurrence. But he's on the porch and he looks back into the room, and without saying so, of course, he's imagining himself dead. By the end of the poem, we realise he's in grief for himself.

I remember reading this and somehow it so expressed how I felt, even though it's a completely different experience. Suddenly I thought, 'I can write now.' I started writing, and it became my book *Carrying the Elephant*. Some of the poems were just four-liners, some of them tiny fragments, others longer. I found I could just talk about what I'd heard or what I'd seen, and some of it was symbolic, and some of it more direct. I thought, 'I can do this. This is saying how I feel, but without saying how I feel.'

I started reading your book Many Different Kinds of Love *on a Tube journey. It's about your experience of being very seriously ill in hospital with COVID-19, and the book begins with the early part of the pandemic in 2020, when none of us knew what was going on. We've moved on now, because life moves on – but even though your language is always very understated, I started crying on the Tube reading it. It immediately conjured up the terror of that time, and how little we understood about what was happening.*

Yes. I'd never want to condemn somebody for using emotion words. Sometimes people can do it stunningly and brilliantly, particularly in song – but I just found that distanced way of writing it very effective. In that book I also used the letters that the nurses wrote to me while I was ill. They're so overwhelming in their kindness and simplicity: 'You can do it!' They didn't know me – they just had this bunch of people on the ward, and they were trying to save our lives, and experiencing nearly half of us dying.

One of the last letters, from a Jamaican nurse, says, 'God bless.' I'm not religious but every time I read that, I'm overwhelmed by it. She's come from thousands of miles away and she's speaking to a complete stranger. It's so moving, even though I've read it a hundred times.

Mary Norris, non-fiction writer and copy editor

You have a joy in the nuts and bolts of language, which obviously was important when you were a copy editor at the New Yorker, *but it also really shines through your own writing. How do you feel when you're working with language?*

I get great sensual pleasure from sentences, from reading them and from crafting them. If there's a twist that makes the last beat of a sentence a little bit funny or ironic, I'll go for that every time. I like associations; I like getting just the right word that reflects some other word that I've already used.

I also enjoy that in my reading. The kind of copy-editing that I did meant always reading something at least twice: first for the content and a second time because, especially if the writer was good, I'd get involved and I'd forget to look for mistakes. I never regretted reading something an extra time, because I had always missed something, so it enhanced my respect for what you can do with words. I especially like subtle things – you can tell when something has been really carefully put together. It's almost sculptural, and it blooms in different places. A really good writer will give everything extra resonance.

I'm trying to get to the bottom of what exactly the relationship of language is to good writing – and I suppose it is in those tiny decisions that bring something extra out of a sentence, where you're deciding which is exactly the right word, how you want to punctuate this, and so on.

Yes, I think it is the little calibrations. Word order and word choice are paramount, certainly more important than punctuation. If the words are not in the right order, you can put in all the semicolons you like and it doesn't move the piece along the way that it should.

I don't like writing that's show-offy, but I really like the right word, and sometimes I learn a new word from something I'm reading. It'll be part of a series, maybe, where the writer seems to be searching as she writes, and will make a little pile-up of words and then finally come to the right one. I may never have heard or read it before, but in the context, I can tell what it means. So when a thing is beautifully written, of course I appreciate that – but if it has a lot of adjectives and adverbs in it, I'll want to take some of them out.

Did you ever have a tug of war with writers about changes that you thought were important?

I had a policy: if something bothered me, and they didn't like the change that I suggested, I would suggest something else. If it still didn't fly, I'd try one more time, and then I'd give up, because it was clear that they wanted it the way they wanted it, and there was something I was missing.

The only time I remember an issue getting a little ugly was not about word choice – it was about typography. The writer was making a visual joke on the page, and he wanted to put something in boldface. One of the things that you get sensitive to as a copy editor is readability, and boldface is a thing for gossip columns – making a name jump out. I thought the joke was clear already, so I kept trying to get him to lose it, and saying that we didn't ever use boldface. He said, 'Don't you ever want to do something new and different?' This is pretty awful of me, but I grumbled that I could do what I wanted once he'd left the office. He got so mad.

How did you resolve it?

He got his way. That's how it works: the writer should get his way. Something appeared in boldface that wouldn't normally appear in boldface, and nothing happened. No one complained, the world didn't end. I even repaired my relationship with that writer.

Do you think that all of those years of reading and working alongside wonderful writers has improved your own writing?

Absolutely. I absorbed a lot just by osmosis. One of the things I frequently did was suggest changes in word order – transpositions – to give a sentence the most power it could possibly have. It was from reading good writers that I learnt how to do that. The point is to keep the reader reading, right? Good writers have the momentum, as well as the right words.

Why do you think that this level of precision is important?

I think it's good to show that you've lavished enough attention on the writing – certainly as much attention as you expect the reader to pay. The mechanics of it have always meant a lot to me, and it might be simply a form of procrastination: grooming the prose because you don't want to let it go yet. But there is something about it being well cared for that I think carries over to a reader. That's one of the things that people take from the *New Yorker*, a famously perfectionist magazine.

Is part of it about showing respect?

Definitely. At the *New Yorker* the care that went into it – with punctuation, maybe with boldface once in a while, but mostly with the right word and making sure everything was spelled right – was all to give the reader the experience that the writer intended. Of course, you could write something with no punctuation at all and just let the reader figure it out. That's another approach, and I think it's valid – readers are adults, they can take care of themselves, and the writer might want some ambiguity – but I'm now trained to make sure that the message gets across as clearly as possible.

Do you think you can be a wonderful writer if you don't have the strongest grasp of spelling, grammar and punctuation?

I do. I like published things to show that somebody has paid attention to detail, but I don't think you need to do that initially. A lot of good writers are challenged by spelling, or they might always use a dash when they want some kind of stop, and the sentence might go on forever – but the attention to detail can come later. It can also come from someone else: an editor.

Richard Ford, a novelist who won a Pulitzer Prize, is dyslexic. It meant that when he was growing up he had trouble reading, and what he learnt to do was take his time – if he read slowly, and looked at the words or even the letters until they settled in the right order, he could do it. Once you know that about him, and read something he's written, and you know how much went into getting these jumbling letters into the right sentence, then you realise that this is a writer who has really been sculpting. There's almost tactile work going on in the words, and it's so compelling that every time I read a sentence I go back and read it again.

7

How do we survive the rewrite?

'A writer is someone who goes back to
the shit first draft and makes it better, and then
goes back again and again and again.'

SATHNAM SANGHERA, journalist, novelist
and non-fiction writer

When I ask professional writers about their first drafts, more often than not they use the word 'mess'. 'Garbage' and 'vomit' also crop up. Some have told me that their finished works bear almost no resemblance to the early stages.

I can tell you from my experience that it's unbelievable how many times an author has to revisit their own manuscript. Editing is a purgatory dream-sequence of repetitive and fine-grained work – a whack-a-mole dotting and crossing of infinite 'i's and 't's. If you want to be a writer, choose a topic you love, because you'll spend an incredible amount of time with it. Prepare to worry at a particular paragraph over months or years, and then maybe even delete it. Prepare to slog.

It's liberating, I think, to accept that this is just how it goes. The knowledge that you will definitely have to polish and rewrite frees you from any obligation to produce something readable on your first attempt, and that is a useful antidote to the self-conscious mind. It tells you that the initial writing phase of a project is not the phase when it has to be good, and that anything can be fixed later if you're prepared to show up for the fixing.

It's helpful to hear this from established writers, because we don't tend to see other people's works in progress, so it's natural to assume that what ends up a masterpiece was a masterpiece all along. The cardinal rule is never to compare your fledgling story with the finished products of the writers you admire. (You will, obviously. But don't.) Imagine trying to build a five-star hotel if you'd never seen a building site. 'This can't be right,' you'd think, horrified. 'There's dust everywhere and a dangerous hole where the golden staircase should be.' You'd be more likely to persevere if you understood that the Ritz was once a mess too.

There is also a point in every editing process when the writer has to let someone else come to the work fresh and tell them how it is. That's not easy: the essayist and performer David Sedaris admits in these pages to 'burning with shame' at the response of his sister and boyfriend to something he was working on, and that's after decades of success. Well-judged feedback, however, can have an enormous positive impact on the standard of the work, and the greatest asset a writer can hope for is a skilled and honest editor (a literary agent often also takes this role) who understands what they're trying to do.

What's tricky is that constructing something solid usually involves destruction along the way. You're building the staircase, but then you're trying to be very honest with yourself about how it looks and functions. The fact is that it's a wonky deathtrap, so if you're brave and you have high standards, you knock it down and you try again. Then you knock it down a second time, if necessary.

That process is hard to commit to on a large scale. I don't mind cutting a flabby paragraph of a 1,200-word article – easy come, easy go. I know from my attempts to write a novel, however, that the prospect of cutting three weak chapters or an entire character is more painful. (Sometimes when a cut is really worrying, I put the removed material into another document in case I need to reinstate it later. Then I forget the document exists.)

Luckily, you're often rewarded with the immediate feeling that the work has improved, and even your manuscript seems relieved. And though I'm complaining, the truth is that I love to edit, because each swipe of red ink through a redundant phrase is so satisfying. I do it mostly on paper, and after periods of what John Lanchester described as the 'hand-to-hand combat' of writing, it's pleasant to sit at a safe distance and take stock.

It feels endless, however. You know you will reach a point where you cannot improve it any more – but you can't accurately judge when that will happen. The deeper you get into a project, the more that yet-to-be-done labour expands before your eyes, like some awful fractal. It can feel sickening, but it's only the project coming to life and asserting itself, which is healthy. Eventually, the hard edges of your book or screenplay emerge, you see some mirage of the finished thing, and your confidence begins to return. The process is so mundane, so toilsome – and yet in the end, it feels miraculous.

When I interview authors, they describe projects that took one, two, five or ten years to complete and release into the world. I used to listen and be glad they stuck with it, but I also wondered if it was really worthwhile – all that effort, that dedication, just for Carol from the Cotswolds to read it and write 'Not for me' next to a one-star Amazon rating. Looked at from afar, the scale of work seems irrational, and you could quite easily talk yourself out of trying; many aspiring writers do, and I suppose I did too, for a while. What kind of idiot would willingly choose such a task, when there is almost certainly nobody asking them to do it? I didn't want to write 200,000 words just to end up, eventually, with 80,000 that weren't terrible.

My perspective on this changed when I started actually doing the work. What I discovered is that once you're deep into a long project, you really don't care that you wasted eighteen months beforehand exploring other versions that didn't go anywhere. The person who did that seems like an acquaintance you've lost touch with, and you're not living in the time that you threw away at the beginning. You only value the manuscript you're looking at right now, which has become a breathing, growing organism. You desperately want it to live and thrive.

So you print it all off again, and you get out your red pen, and you have another try at turning it into something so good that nobody will ever imagine it was once a mess. We all spend the many hours of our lives doing something. Why not use them for this wonderful, difficult miracle?

Wendy Cope, poet

The thing about poets is that they're people who are prepared to work on something very small and get it just right.

Obsessive, is it fair to say?

Oh, yes.

Mona Arshi, poet, novelist and essayist

I'd never send a poem out to a magazine immediately after I'd written it. Poetry wisdom says you're supposed to leave it for about three months – actually, six, but I can never leave it that long – and then when you peruse it again, it's almost as though all the energy has leaked out of it. At that point, I can understand all the issues very, very clearly. All my blind spots and the stuff that doesn't feel true – it's all exposed after three months of sitting on its own.

It's as though when we're reading something on the day or the week that we've been writing it, we're bringing ourselves to the page as well. We can't quite distinguish between what we've written and what is happening in our hearts. Then when we come back to it later, we're clean of it, so we can see the page clearly.

It's true. I also think that with poetry in particular, because you are so exposed – because you are working in this tiny space – it's like panning for gold. The good stuff comes to the surface if you spend enough time with this imaginary sieve, and hopefully only the good stuff will rise to the surface, but if any of it is fool's gold, the reader can hear it and see it. With prose, you can get away with a dodgy few pages; a poem will upend itself with an ill-judged line break or even a misused comma.

George Saunders, short-story writer

The role of cutting is really underestimated. I think I get my voice, such as it is, by cutting things out. We often think writing is, 'Oh, I'm going to finally inhabit my true self and sing at the top of my lungs with no inhibition!', but you do that and you go, 'Ugh, that sounds like everybody else.' Then you start cutting it back.

That's interesting, because what's the basis for cutting? It's every bit as strong an aesthetic position as when you put something in – maybe even more so. We all know what a normal sentence sounds like – a habitual, almost lazy sentence; the difference between that and a style-inflected sentence is in the micro-choosing that a person can learn to do, which really tells us everything about her.

It's also an anti-writer's block formula, to say, 'Just write down any old crap.' If you have a powerful ear, you can prune away at that mediocre thing until it starts to sound a little strange and good.

Would you tell me how redrafting works for you?

Yeah – and I would underscore 'for me', because I think I'm a little excessive in this regard, but my editing process is to approach the text as if I haven't seen it before. That in itself might be about eighty per cent of the job – learning to do that in a convincing way, so you're not attached to what you did yesterday, or your thematic ideas; you're just reading it as if you picked up the book on a bus. Then you're watching to see whether your mind is leaning into it with pleasure or pulling back in revulsion. Over the course of your career, I think you can get better at doing that on a really fine level – you can feel a slight aversion or attraction.

There's a moment when the thinking mind wants to get involved. It's up there going, 'It's about patriarchy!' but what you really want to do is turn that down. Just be directly keyed into the pleasure, or whatever you want to call it. Your hand will say, 'Ah, that phrase is slightly repetitive,' and cut it – or you'll blurt out a phrase that's more interesting. Your mind is interacting with the text in a really intimate way, and so for me the whole thing is to dial back that conceptual, controlling, lecturing part of my mind that knows what my story is about, and let this other mysterious voice dominate.

What I've found over the years is that the mysterious voice is really smart, and it knows all about character development and theme and plot and politics, but it just doesn't wear it on its shoulder – so for me, writing is more meditative than intellectual.

The other thing that works is just to do it over and over again. It makes me feel a little better about making mistakes – if I screw it up today, I'll fix it tomorrow. Also, in a way I've never been able to articulate, it gives me access to a better part of myself. There's a funnier, more honest part of me in my prose, especially when it's rewritten like this, than is present if you met me in person. In person I'm about as funny as your third-funniest uncle, and I'm not really that honest. I tend to be a little hyperbolic and a little Pollyannaish – I don't like to say anything negative. But as a writer, when you see a part in your own prose that's dishonest, you fix it, and your honesty just went up a notch, and *that* person is more interesting. That's what I really love about this job.

Sathnam Sanghera, journalist, novelist and non-fiction writer

A writer is someone who survives the horror of the first draft. Ernest Hemingway said, 'The first draft of anything is shit.' A lot of people write their first thing and think, 'Oh my god, that's terrible. I'm not a writer.' I think anyone can be a writer. A writer is someone who goes back to the shit first draft and makes it better, and then goes back again and again and again.

Brandon Taylor, novelist

I have absolute faith in my ability to produce words. I try not to be precious about the words I have on the page, because I know that I can always throw them out and make more. I'm not the kind of writer who thinks I can only write fifty words, and I have to chisel them out of a mountain, and they have to be perfect when they come.

Graham Norton, novelist

In the morning, I go over everything I wrote in the last session and polish it as best I can. Then in the afternoon, I'll start a new bit, and write until 5.30 p.m., maybe, before I hear the clink of ice and I'm out of there.

I have spoken to a lot of authors who try to resist going back over the previous day's work, because they feel that you can get stuck in one section – but it sounds like you're quite disciplined about doing that and then pushing forward.

Yes. I remember we had a history teacher at school, and he

began every lesson with 'As I was saying last time . . .'. We got stuck
in the Middle Ages for about three years, with him refreshing what
he'd done the week before. So I try not to get too bogged down.
Occasionally you go back and you realise, 'This is rubbish. This
does not require polishing – this requires knocking down and
rebuilding.' But it's all for the good. You're still working towards
the best book you know how to write, and in the end, all of the
work is valuable. It's never wasted time.

Meg Wolitzer, novelist

I write the beginning of a novel with as little hesitation as I can. I
try to write with pleasure, and it's like I'm walking around with a
secret world inside me, thinking about these people and this idea,
and that can be exciting. But I do find myself revising the opening
a lot, not to perfect it, but because I have a feeling that it will serve
as an emotional template for me. What do I want the book to feel
like? I want that uneasiness or humour or depth to be there in the
beginning, and for the book to be supersaturated with it. I don't
want to move ahead until I know that it's there.

I feel that a writer's world should have a certain temperature.
I find it miraculous that you can read one line of something and
know it's by Margaret Atwood, even though she may have various
styles – it's her sensibility. Have I provided that? Or does what's
on the page feel a little bit generic?

Having reassured myself that the work includes the strange,
uneasy or funny feeling I've been having about these characters,
I try to plunge forward and amass as much as possible, because
otherwise it would be very easy to become fetishistic about a small
section, and to get stuck on it. I think that the more you have to

work with, the more you find things that connect and will carry you through.

When you've got a complete draft, and you're picking it up again to read, what are you looking for?

The great thing that we have is revision – even though it's not at all sexy. It involves repetition, and staring; it's almost like looking at yourself in the mirror up close, examining your pores. It's not the exciting part, and it's not really packed with invention. I think, though, that in those moments, if you're being really honest, you can see where you've failed yourself – and I so often have.

There are so many things to do. When I finish a novel, I often look at it and think, 'Who wrote that? Did I hire people to come in here?' – because there were so many things to take care of, and I actually took care of them. Of course, it takes a long time. I examine the work as if with a jeweller's loupe. Does this language carry the weight? Sometimes the weakest writing for me, I've noticed, seems to hold the weakest ideas – so it may be, in fact, that the idea hasn't been thought through enough. Then it's not about saying it better, but about reinterrogating what I am trying to say.

I read dialogue aloud – key moments, at least. I like the idea of letting people talk in a book, and not being intrusive and stopping things when you want to show the way the light looks. Did I let them talk in a way that didn't just get across my point, but also showed who they are and how they are with each other? The best way to reveal character is sometimes to show people together; it uncovers things that people don't want to present about themselves, so dialogue is an enormous part of it. There are moments when I hear my husband outside my office, and I'm embarrassed because I know I was reading aloud in that voice to myself – no matter how hard I try, it always has this very particular cadence – but the only way to know if it's OK is by listening.

When I started writing, I used a little electric typewriter. It was a very, very different experience. I used Wite-Out to correct mistakes, so it was almost like doing a craft – as if I was painting on the page. I spent so much time changing things that I didn't like, and writing them in by hand when the white stuff dried, that I was very close to the work. I could memorise it. It's so different now. You get rid of whole swathes of prose because you look at it and say, 'That's shit.' Maybe some of it is worth saving, but in the moment and the rhythm, you get rid of it, and it's gone. I find a little bit of melancholy in that, because I had the previous experience, which was labour-intensive, but you really saw what was there. Sometimes you could even see what you'd gotten rid of. You'd hold it up to the light and think, 'Well, maybe I want that back.'

Sometimes I'll think something's done but my editor might feel differently, and raise an issue that I couldn't see. Writing can be like those Magic Eye pictures – you stare and stare, and you can't see it for the longest period of time. I don't know what changes in the brain that makes you suddenly able to see something, but it's incredible when it happens. It's like psychoanalysis: you're lying there and you think you're doing nothing, but you're looking at it, looking at it, looking at it. Then you realise, 'Oh, the reason I put this in, without fully understanding it, is so that it could connect to that.' That is when things get exciting – when you find connections in your own work that you hadn't understood. Objects in particular can serve as links between people, and take on meaning later that they didn't have initially.

How do you feel about revising in collaboration with an editor?

I have a very close working relationship with my US editor, Sarah McGrath, and we've worked together for a really long time. At the beginning of each book, we have a big lunch and talk about what I want to do – so that when the book is finished, her responses are not to some phantom thing, but to what I said I wanted. The desires of the writer, the imperative of the writer, remain central, which is really important to me. 'I wanted a particular sensation, and I wanted to explore this question – does it seem like I did that?' Maybe she'll suggest some ways I could do it that might work better.

If I trust the person, I will always really listen – but ultimately, it's the writer's book, and you want it to convey who you were as a writer at that moment.

André Aciman, novelist, memoirist and essayist

I usually write too much, but I'm always very happy to remove things. If you mark something I've written as unnecessary, I'll go with it. I think I'm the easiest writer on the planet to edit – I'll do anything you say. 'This word is wrong? Fine.' Out it goes.

I'm very insecure, that's why. I don't trust myself, so I always look for another pair of eyes to give me direction and tell me, 'Of course you're wrong, André. This is how you should have done it.'

Listen to your editors, if you have good editors. Bad editors will like what you do – they will love it. That's usually the sign of a bad editor.

David Sedaris, essayist and performer

It's always a mistake to share something before it's finished. I did it yesterday. I read something to my sister and my boyfriend – and the response was as though I had shit in my pants. I was burning with shame by the end of it. Amy was too polite to say anything, but Hugh said, 'I didn't laugh once' – which he didn't need to say, because I had noticed that. I thought, 'OK, well, that's what I get for reading something before it's done.' It was a good way of putting a nail in it, so then I can move on.

You do hone your essays on tour, though, when you're reading them to audiences again and again – so in a sense, the first time you perform it, it's not in its final form. What's the difference between the thing that's ready to share and the thing that isn't?

Well, the thing that I read yesterday wasn't finished. I took five or six essays on my most recent tour, including one that I wrote about my friend Dawn, and it is pretty different now from when I first read it – but even at that point, I thought, 'This is the best thing I've written in years,' and the audience really liked it. The tour lasted almost two months, and I still made changes throughout, just to see if this worked or that worked. Now the *New Yorker* has it, and if they take it, then there'll be more rewriting to be done with them, but I wanted it in a shape that I was happy with before they read it.

I sent it to my book editor, and one of her suggestions was to cut out the biggest laugh in the whole piece, which I wasn't about to do. That's the good thing about having an opportunity to read something out loud, because you know what's your biggest laugh.

And actually, most writers don't get that direct feedback – you have the benefit of being a performer too.

I often feel like the audience are my editor. If they cough, that's them telling me that if this were on the page, they would be skimming. But I like different kinds of laughs as well, and there are so many different kinds: there's the 'I can't believe he just said that' laugh, and the 'I can't believe I'm laughing at that' laugh. There's a groan, which I am always happy to have.

The audience tell me everything. If the lights were on, and they could see me looking at them, they wouldn't tell me everything, because they would want to please me – they're polite people and so they would have a rictus of pleasure on their faces, on the off chance that I caught their eye. They're in the dark and I can't see them though, so they can cough, or just not laugh – or they can boo, which has happened.

What did they boo at?

I wrote an essay about hitting kids, and how I think it's a good idea. I'm not talking about beating your children with belts – I was just saying that there were six kids in my family and we got slapped across the face all the time. My parents didn't have time to stop everything and say, 'Time out, young man – you go to your room.' They didn't have time, so they slapped someone across the face and moved on. It didn't kill me.

I read it all over the country, which was interesting. I got booed in Massachusetts, but people went nuts in the south – they were more than happy to hit their kids there, and they were cheering. Then someone wrote to me that obviously I'm suffering from PTSD.

Would you tell me a little bit about your revision process for an essay?

Usually with the first draft, everything goes into it – and then I'm carving an essay out of it. Let's say I've got twenty pages;

I think, 'OK, there's an essay within these pages. If I chip this off, and if I chip this off, then I can get to what the essay is about.'

Because I read in front of an audience, I want things to move. I started inviting young writers to open for me, and a lot of the things that they write just don't move. Maybe it's an essay about a person's feelings, or maybe the characters don't have a name or a want – that can be excruciating for a live audience. On paper, it might be different, but if you're going to be in front of people, things have to move. I think about that, and I think, 'OK, let's put more dialogue here.'

I like to see famous people in the wild, so recently I wrote an essay about the stars I've seen. I read it out loud on stage one night, but I got tangled up in listing all the names. The next night I took half of them out, and it worked 100 times better, and then I could add things and make the essay about something more. So, I saw Cher at Dover Street Market in London, and I couldn't shut up about it – everywhere I went that day, I said, 'I just saw Cher!' Then at one place where I stopped, this kid who was working the espresso machine said, 'Who's Cher?' and I thought, 'When young people don't know your stars, that means you're going to die.'

Reading out loud helped me learn that the essay needed something like that. That's what's great about having forty-six opportunities to read something to an audience.

Charlie Brooker, screenwriter

Usually I'll send my first draft straight to a colleague, who will pick it apart, and I can't help but get really defensive. No one wants to take feedback on their work. I still hate it, but it's probably more than half the job of being a writer: getting notes from people and being annoyed and defensive, and then having to go away and simmer. Then you think, 'Ah fuck, they're right.' There's nothing worse.

I've got better at recognising that they're right while it's coming out of their mouth. You have to swallow your natural fear. In that moment, you're ashamed, and you're afraid that you're not going to be able to do it properly, or that it's going to be too much work, but you have to go through all of that. It doesn't mean that you have to do what they're saying, but a lot of the time they're onto something.

Somebody else described it much better than me – they said it's a bit like a patient going to see the doctor. The patient might say, 'My leg really hurts.' It doesn't mean you saw the leg off. They're just saying, 'I've noticed a problem,' and your job is not to deny it, but to work out how to make it better. It might be that they're saying, 'I don't like this character,' while really the problem is something else – but you shouldn't just dismiss what they're saying out of hand.

My colleague will read it and she'll write a load of notes, during which time, if I reread it, I've got my own thoughts about what works and what doesn't. She'll be saying, 'What's this about?' and 'I didn't like this bit' and so on and so forth, and I'm going, 'Well yes, OK – it's very first drafty!' I feel completely exposed, but then I usually think of a solution. It's an unpleasant process, but it always makes things better.

That's the first draft. Then you'll get to a point where you're happy to show it to Netflix, or use it to try to interest directors or cast members, that sort of thing, so it's a bit more polished, but you will still get notes back. Netflix will have their own thoughts, and they're never prescriptive. They never say, 'You mustn't do this,' but they might go, 'Why has the cowboy got the bum problem?' Then you go through the process again. You either think of a solution or you defend it.

Once there's a producer and a director on board, you have the whole conversation again, so now it's, 'Well hang on, we can't go to Droitwich to film this. Droitwich is incredibly expensive! Does this bit have to be set in a boat? Do we need this montage?' Often a lot of it is finding ways to save money and make the schedule as efficient as possible, and that's a very, very, very annoying but also necessary part of the process.

Once you cast it, sometimes you'll rewrite the part depending on who you've cast to tweak it more to their voice. Then you'll have other problems that might come up during the shoot, where you're running out of time and so you have to drop scenes, or an actor gets sick, or the location burns down – so you rewrite it again. Then the final rewrite is in the edit suite, which I think a lot of writers don't get into. I'm very lucky because I can walk into the edit whenever I want and not leave until I'm happy. I think that's the most important draft.

People often say this, that the final rewrite is in the edit suite, and I'm always slightly confused – surely all you can really do at that point is cut things out or change the order that they happen in?

No, you can do lots. You can cut to the back of someone's head and write a whole new line for them. In the *Black Mirror* episode 'San Junipero', there's a huge bit of that, but no one ever notices it. There's a whole chunk where there was something that didn't make sense, so we recorded additional dialogue.

You spot it all over the place. I was watching *The Crown* the other day, and there was a very clear bit where it cuts to Princess Anne listening to Prince Philip, and off camera he says something like, 'Well, we're going to do this documentary because it's the first time that the royal family has ever . . . and this is the year 1968 and Harold Wilson is in charge!' So you can do that sort of thing, you can make things very clear. Often if you've cut something else out, you have to do that so it still makes sense, but you can also totally alter the tone and the mood of what's happening. You can find a shot of an actor doing something with their face that communicates something that either wasn't in the script, or there wasn't a line of dialogue that communicated it. Depending on where you place the focus, you can completely alter the meaning or the feel of a scene, and that's very important.

Whenever I speak to someone who's getting into scriptwriting, I tell them: get in the edit suite if you can. You're the last person they want in there, but the reason you should be is that it's amazing how often directors and editors don't really refer back to the script while they cut it.

You'll go in and you'll think, 'Something's not quite right about this – what's going on? This person's just murdered someone and they should be really worried, I remember that . . .'. You'll look back at the script and it's full of descriptions like, 'She looks shiftily from side to side with beads of sweat forming on her brow.' You say to the editor, 'Where's all of this . . .?' and they're like, 'Oh yeah!' You've written this big book of instructions. You can go back and make sure that the edit is adhering to your notion of how things should play out, but you can also completely alter things very quickly.

Jesse Armstrong, screenwriter

Often when I'm leading a writers' room, I retell everyone the story of the show. 'Here we are at episode five. In episode one, they all get together for a party, and this goes wrong. Then this happens . . .'. It's very useful, because especially in a group creative environment, different writers hook onto different bits of the story. 'Oh, I thought the main thing was going to be the birthday cake.' 'No, the main thing for me is this relationship between these two minor characters . . .'. So you get to broaden out the world, because you can discuss both things that seemed like they might be the heart of the episode, and you shape the idea in the retelling.

When I'm repitching the story, looking at the faces of the other writers, I can also see when I've reached a part that snags in the room. Then you can hone in and say, 'That part is shit, isn't it? Why?' Often the answer is that we've forced it, because we want to get from A to C. Well, what if we didn't have to get to C? What's the painful, difficult, interesting, funny, true thing that would naturally happen next? Often, that conversation releases you from this bondage of having decided, 'Oh, we need them all to end up in the delicatessen.' Then you can start to feel an incredible freedom, though you might also feel an incredible terror of not knowing where the story's going.

I think one thing that really improves any writer's work is learning not to ignore it when you feel something snagging, even though it's terrifying. You don't get better until you admit to yourself, 'This isn't working and I'm going to have to fix it.'

Yes, it's tempting to try not to look at it. Talking things through is helpful. You begin to solve seventy per cent of your problems as soon as you can articulate them: 'There's not enough jeopardy in the middle,' or 'This is not very clear,' or 'This is too clear, and there's not enough intrigue.' Often the solution arises when you realise that you've overcommitted to something that doesn't really have to happen.

When I go back to revise one of my own scripts, I'm asking myself certain questions: 'Should this bit even be here? Can I just get rid of it? If it's not working, why not?' If there is a part of it that is working, I drive towards that. Cut away the flesh around it, and get to that great dynamic, or joke, or painful thing. Expand the part that does work, the bit that feels like it's got some creative heat to it and is getting you through the scene – rather than try to pump life into the bits that feel dead. For me, it's often about looking for character relationships that have an interesting spark.

The difficult thing is when the bits that you like don't help the story. You need to be very willing to chuck something out even if you enjoyed writing it, because otherwise you can be trying to protect something that's killing the whole entity. Try to expunge anything that doesn't feel true to your world, or feels like a cliché.

Sophie Mackintosh, novelist

I find the concept of the bay leaf very helpful when I'm redrafting. The bay leaf is something you have in your work – a scene, or a description, or a character that you're attached to – but eventually you realise you have to take it out. You think, 'I really love this scene, and I don't want to remove it, but I don't need it any more. It's not working.' That's fine. It served its purpose – it helped you get to this point, and now you can let it go. It's the bay leaf.

Ayòbámi Adébáyò, novelist

For a very long time, I didn't think that it was valid to keep going over the same thing again and again. I thought that if it doesn't come out well the first or the second time I try it, then it's not good enough, or I'm not good enough. It's really been helpful to me to trust that I can go back repeatedly and make my work a little better.

For me, the first draft is really messy. I have notes in capital letters – a scene might end with, 'THERE NEEDS TO BE A CONVERSATION ABOUT X AND Y.' So the second draft is about going back to think through those questions that I asked myself. I go from the beginning to the end again, and by the third draft, I'm thinking about how things connect to each other, and the structure. Which chapter should actually be the first chapter? It's the architecture of the book that makes it feel seamless, and that's one of the things I really like when I'm reading – to have things flow into each other in a way that is almost natural or necessary.

Once the third draft is done, I start going through chapter by chapter and paragraph by paragraph. I usually have three documents open at that point: the manuscript, and then two blank documents. From the manuscript, I take no more than 1,000 words at a time and paste them into document two, and read it from top to bottom a few times.

At this stage, is it a matter of making the language as elegant and as tight as it can be?

A lot of other things will come up just because you're going over it again, and you realise that someone was fifty years old and now they're forty-five. But really, yes, I'm reading it for language and how one paragraph flows into another, and how a chapter begins and ends and what each sentence is saying. This is the stage at which I'm likely to read paragraphs to myself, read dialogue out loud, just to get a feel of the sound. I'm looking very closely at everything, sentence by sentence.

In the second document, once I'm done working on each paragraph, I change its font. Then I read it one last time, and I copy it to the third document, which is now the new manuscript.

I'm impressed by how painstaking that is. Do you at any point think, 'God, I'm so bored of looking at this book that I can't even see it straight any more?'

Absolutely. It usually happens at least two or three times before the book is published, and I just take a break. Sometimes it's a month, sometimes all I need is a week, and I try to work on something else, or I get immersed in a really big novel. I read something that is 500 pages long, and then I can come back to my book and it can feel new. But yes, there's a point closer to publication when I think, 'I cannot read this again.' And then I do.

Rumaan Alam, novelist

The first draft of my novel *Leave the World Behind* ended with Clay and Amanda outside of the house, leaning against the car, prepared to drive away, and the lights in the house went out. That was the end of the book. My agent and the editor were both like, 'What the fuck is this?'

That's a great note from a reader. It was like, oh, right. The book is not done. I was building to uncertainty, but that's too much uncertainty. It was really helpful, and I was able to recalibrate. I then realised how I needed the book to end: on a question. I couldn't identify that until I had written that first bad ending.

Emily St. John Mandel, novelist and screenwriter

One of my core values as a writer is velocity, which means that a lot of material that I think is good ends up falling by the wayside. There were entire chapters of *Station Eleven* that I eliminated in revisions. Sometimes a chapter or a character can be really good and work really well in and of itself, but it doesn't serve the book. It slows things down or it's too much detail about a secondary character – so I kill darlings all the time.

I'm often able to use them in a later book, though. On a couple of occasions, I've cut out a backstory or an entire character, and used that as the basis for a short story years later. I wrote a scene where a woman is telling another woman's fortune on the porch at a party, and I pushed that for, I think, two books. It was in *Station Eleven*, then it was in *The Glass Hotel*, then it finally landed in *Sea of Tranquility*.

It's very encouraging to think that things you like don't have to be completely killed.

Yeah, you might just think of it as cold storage.

Let's talk about editing and revising your work – would you talk me through your process?

Sure. The background's important here, which is that I never write from an outline. That has pluses and minuses – it means the first draft is messy. The prose itself doesn't change very much from the first draft to the final draft, but the structure will be a mess, and there will be a lot of extraneous material and characters who are underdeveloped. My girlfriend's been reading a draft of the novel I'm working on now, and her comment was, 'All the characters sound like you.' She's absolutely correct. It's a first draft and they're all placeholders. That's the kind of thing that will change in revision.

So I begin with the first draft, and I generally revise it three times in straightforward, beginning-to-end fashion. Of course, you start out with massive problems, and then the problems get smaller and smaller the further you go. I'm asking myself, 'Is my attention dragging a little bit? Do I need an entire chapter of back-story, or might this be a paragraph? Can I eliminate description?' I don't describe what my characters look like, because I want my reader to fill in the gap with their imagination, and I feel like that will make them more invested. How short can the book possibly be and still function? That's a big part of it for me.

Then the most useful trick I've learnt for revising is a random-page-order edit, which sounds a little bit crazy. I noticed that when I took random pages off the printer and started reading in the middle of the book, I would catch issues that I'd somehow missed in four previous rounds of revision. My theory is that if you've been working on a manuscript for a very long time, your brain knows what's coming and will skim over problems and fill in gaps. It gets to the point where you can have a typo in your first sentence, and you can't see it. What I've been doing for the last several books is to revise, say, page 250, and then page four, and then page seventy-eight, and jump all over the place within the manuscript. I put a check mark in the corner of each page as I read it. I catch all kinds of problems that I'd otherwise have missed. Reading it out of order, it's like your brain is forced to do a hard reset on what you're looking at. That's my most valuable trick.

After those revisions, I try to find three early readers I trust to give constructive feedback. I want them to tell me what's wrong with the book without being egregiously mean about it. It isn't always novelists – sometimes it's friends who are booksellers or who work in publishing, or I gave *Sea of Tranquility* to a friend who's a screenwriter, because screenwriters know about plot, and that was a particular concern with this book. I'll get notes from those readers, and then I revise based on those notes, and then I send it to my agent. She always has editorial notes, and once I satisfy those, then she sends it to my editors and sells it, and I get their notes back.

Do you think it's possible to rewrite or edit too much in your quest for velocity? Could you damage the book?

Absolutely – that's always a possibility. I've had the experience of being an early reader for friends, where I'll read a draft and I can see maybe one or two small things that need to be changed, but it's amazing. Then I'll read the next draft, and it's been reworked, and it's not as good. That's something that I fear, because I don't think it's possible to see when you pass that tipping point, but it's definitely there.

I have three editors, which is a very unusual circumstance – one at my US publisher, one in Canada and one in the UK. The three of them are pretty formidable. I was afraid at first that it would turn into a nightmare of editing by committee, and of course the apocalyptic scenario is that your editors won't agree, but I've done three books with them and we're essentially on the same wavelength. I have no idea what goes on behind the scenes, but they get their stories straight, and I get epic emails from the three of them, like twelve pages of single-spaced editorial notes. I trust them deeply. I love that there are three of them, and they make my work so much better.

Will Storr, long-form journalist and author

When I was a young writer, Jon Ronson was a big hero of mine, and I once went to interview him. As I was leaving his lovely house, I said, 'Oh, Jon, do you have any advice for a young writer?' and he said, 'Yes, I've got some advice. Brevity.'

I remember thinking, 'That's shit advice. Brevity? Who wants brevity?' But actually, it was the best advice ever, and it took me about fifteen years to work that out. I wish I could go back and cut 20,000 words each out of my books *The Heretics* and *Selfie*.

Just because you're fascinated by this weird little corner of the thing that's tangentially related to your story doesn't mean everybody else is going to be – and as a writer, you can't rely on your editors to cut that for you, because these days they're editing a million people and they only really edit when something's gone badly wrong. You've got to be your own editor, and I think I really learnt that when I wrote *The Science of Storytelling*. It's short and I could have written at twice the length, but I think one of the things that worked about it was its brevity.

The other good piece of advice – I suppose it's related – was from my editor at *Arena*, a guy called William Drew. He said to me, 'You know, the thing about writing is you don't have to be comprehensive. You don't have to put everything you know in there.' I think that's a mistake that lots of non-fiction writers make. If you're writing properly, the question is not 'How can I get all of this in the book?' but 'What can I get rid of?' Being selective makes for much better reading.

Will Harris, poet and essayist

I revise my work obsessively – and too muchly. I think one of the appeals of poetry, and also its dangers, is that you can just endlessly fiddle with it. You can't fiddle as much in a longer form like a novel. With poems, there's endless room to switch words around and change line breaks, and it gives play to a contained form of insanity. I think of it as a mix between hysteria and paranoia – you're pattern-finding in that paranoid way, but it's hysterical because it's an overflowing of language as well. You're trying to rein it in.

Ruben Östlund, film-maker

For me, there's a risk when too many people are reading your screenplay and saying, 'You should change that, this character is not sympathetic, blah, blah, blah' – all this bullshit that you have to hear if you're a screenwriter. It can take away the core of what you were interested in when you started writing. Sometimes it can take away the uniqueness.

With my earlier films, it was very important that I protected the ideas in the beginning, even though on paper they maybe didn't make sense to somebody who was used to a more traditional way of writing movies. I can fine-tune everything later, but I have to let myself be playful and free when I decide on the content of the film, because otherwise I'm going to censor myself and make my film less unique.

I would advise anybody who is dealing with screenplays not to hope for writing the perfect script. When it comes to why a movie is made or not, so much of it is about social connections. Try not to rewrite, rewrite, rewrite too much, because you can get away from the core, and the reason that you started the project.

8

How do writers learn?

'You've got to get your hands dirty – you have to be
right there inside the work, in order to make it work.'

MAGGIE O'FARRELL, novelist

A few months after I graduated from university and moved to
London, aged twenty-three, I was introduced to someone
from the same cohort. She asked me what I did, and I explained
that I had a temporary job as assistant to my cousin, who worked
in academic PR, and meanwhile I was applying for magazine
internships and journalism courses. This was not exactly stage one
of a well-thought-out plan; it was a scattergun strategy based on my
best guess at how to be paid for writing. I'd spent my student years
focusing on other things, such as cultivating romantic intrigue,
and at this point I'm not sure I was writing much at all. The need
to find a career had come upon me out of nowhere.

She listened politely and in turn, I asked what she was doing.
'I'm a playwright,' she said. That was the end of the response. I
looked at her, a girl of my own age. She looked back at me. We
looked at each other, and I said, 'Cool.'

I'm a playwright. Not 'I want to be a playwright,' or 'I'm studying playwriting,' or 'I'm hoping to intern at a theatre' – no, she
had claimed her right to write, straight out of the gate. She didn't

qualify it with unnecessary detail either. She was taking herself seriously as a writer in a way that I hadn't yet dared. I was impressed and depressed in equal measure.

I never met her again, but within a few years she was quite famous. It turned out that she'd been writing and producing plays for a while by the time we were introduced, and she ascended quickly afterwards: she knew what she wanted to do, but more importantly, she was already doing it. What I didn't really understand at the time is that doing it – which requires you to confront the possibility that you won't immediately be good at it – is the only way to learn.

Creativity sometimes suffers from association with supernatural talent. We call William Shakespeare a genius, by which we mean someone with an ability that far outstrips the norm – but he also did a hell of a lot of work, immersing himself in the theatre and maintaining a prodigious output. From Nobel Prize winners to pop icons, the very accomplished require dedication and grit. In my twenties, I thought successful people were simply gifted and assured in a way that I wasn't, and maybe they were, but they were also brave enough to get out there and graft despite the risk of failure. The ridiculous fear of not being a genius is, for some of us, a barrier to trying at all.

It's when you push through that barrier that progress can begin. When I speak to writers about what helped them improve, their answers tend to fall into three categories. The most obvious can be loosely described as 'practice'. There is no substitute for writing a lot – but perhaps less obviously, practice also means reading as much as you can. In addition, I believe creatives require a certain amount of time and space to steep in their thoughts about the work, and even about life. (This can be frustrating for people who love us but don't understand how we can stare into space for forty-five minutes and then declare ourselves stressed.)

The second category is interaction with others. This may mean teachers or editors who can share technical advice on the craft – but writing friends and peers are also invaluable. They can both support us and challenge us, because improvement is spurred by the act of being read. Sharing work holds us accountable in a way that writing in secret does not, and regular feedback forces us to keep stretching. It can be painful – as the crime author Amer Anwar recalls: 'You sit there, lip quivering, thinking, "Don't cry!"' – but it's productive.

Finally, there's opportunity and luck. They're not everything, and the comedian James Acaster shares strong views on that in this chapter – but they do help. I mention this because it's not easy to become a professional writer, or even an amateur writer with an audience. Doors don't open as swiftly for some people as for others, as several authors discuss in these pages, and since writers are generally prone to beating themselves up over failure, I think it's important to acknowledge that publishing isn't a meritocracy.

It's also a privilege to have the time and energy to work on something that, let's face it, isn't lucrative. Accessing the imagination requires a level of peace and clear-headedness; it's difficult to be creative during demanding or perilous times. Every writer will at some point find that real life is standing in the way of their progress: if it happens to you, allow it as a temporary detour. Remember that although great writing is achieved by hard work, it is also often supported by a scaffolding of good luck, which might not be with you today, but might come tomorrow – and there are pockets of funding and mentorship programmes out there, waiting to be applied for, which can be transformative.

In practical terms, there are well-worn routes that hit the three categories to help a writer improve. The most formal is the creative-writing course, which provides practice and also interaction with others: alongside assessment by teachers, there's usually workshopping, which involves students reading and offering notes on each other's work. I was very used to getting feedback as a journalist, but when I took my master's degree in creative writing – fourteen years into my career – I found that critically reading other people's stories was as educational as hearing what they thought about mine. Novelists Kiley Reid, Anna Hope and Brandon Taylor are among the writers I've spoken to who have benefited from a degree course.

A degree is expensive, however; the cost can be mitigated by bursaries and scholarships, but it's also not the only path. We're living in a boom time for creative-writing resources that are available cheaply or for free. You can find a local writers' group, or form your own workshop with friends. There are many helpful online communities, newsletters and free courses, and wonderful craft books by Anne Lamott, Stephen King, Nikesh Shukla, Vivian Gornick, Julia Cameron and too many others to list here. There are also residencies and fellowships that aspiring writers can apply for, which can not only ease the financial challenges of creative work, but also provide the structure, consistency and community that speed up progress; novelist Ayọ̀bámi Adébáyọ̀ reflects in these pages on how deeply she benefited from them.

In my first decade of working life, I received an ad hoc journalistic education so rigorous that some days were bruising – but they were exhilarating too. In my second, I've learnt how to write a book, and I did that by writing one. I eventually summoned the courage to get my hands dirty, as novelist Maggie O'Farrell puts it, and that's where any aspiring writer must start.

Kit de Waal, novelist and short-story writer

By my early forties, I'd adopted a little boy who was very ill and I'd given up work for the first time in twenty-something years. He spent loads of time in hospital or asleep at home, and I was bored. I had plumped the cushions to within an inch of their life, I'd redecorated, I'd done the dreaded mother and baby groups, which I loathed – so I thought, 'Well, have a go at writing, because you're a great reader and you were always good at English.'

So I started to write. I loved it, but my god, it was much harder than it seemed. I was staggered to find that I couldn't get the thoughts that were in my heart onto the page very easily at all, and that fascinated me, so I started deconstructing some novels that I liked. I did some short courses, I joined a couple of writing groups, and I took the craft very, very seriously. I knew that if I was going to get better, it was going to be because I was taught.

I did a master's degree. It wasn't very good, it has to be said, but it did give me a year to concentrate on my writing. I was fifty-two by then. I'd been writing for six or seven years very seriously, and by the time I finished the master's, I understood some of the terminology at the very least, and what people meant by point of view, third person, narrative, plot – all of these things that you absolutely have to know as a writer.

So it was about getting the technical side of it straight in your mind.

Yes, and you can't find your own voice unless you do understand something of the craft. There are people who don't do many courses – they just sit down and write their book. Those people will absolutely have spent many years writing though, or at least reading and thinking about reading.

People are really quite snobby about creative-writing degrees. Although mine wasn't very good, I would never tell someone not to do one, if they can afford it – I think the cost is probably the only reason you shouldn't. People say, 'Well, Gustave Flaubert never did a creative-writing degree. Ernest Hemingway never did a creative-writing degree,' but what those men will have done is spend hours and days and weeks writing, and talking about writing with their friends. Many of them didn't work. They dedicated their lives to being writers.

Of course you don't have to do a degree, but you do have to spend the time, and you do need to have some respect for the craft. Even the simplest books are hard to write. It's very healthy to know all the tools of your trade, even if you end up only using one.

When I started as a journalist, I remember being so demoralised by how poor some of my writing was. I could see it was poor, but I couldn't work out how to improve it, and it really did take years of practice before I started to feel that writing was less hard. Is that how you felt in your fiction?

Completely. Oh my god, it was so bad. I was shocked, because in my head it was this beautiful thing, and then I'd try to get it down on the page and it just wasn't working. Flaubert put it beautifully: 'Language is a cracked kettle on which we beat out tunes for bears to dance to, while all the time we long to move the stars to pity.' It is exactly like that. Even when we get it right, sometimes we don't absolutely nail what it is to be grieving or lost or in love. That's one of the reasons why there is still space for other writers to talk about those things, because none of us do it perfectly or entirely. There's always another way.

You've done a lot to push for more inclusivity in publishing. What are the changes that you would most like to see to give more people the opportunity to become authors?

I would like to see a more expansive idea in the industry of what a novel is and who writes what. Very often when I talk about working-class people having the chance to write, people think I'm saying we should have more stories about tower blocks and people on the margins, and the woman who works in Asda – let's look at her life. That isn't what I'm saying at all. What I'm saying is that the working-class writer should be able to write whatever they want and have the opportunity to get published. A lot of that depends on having networks and time, and being introduced to people, and being able to do a course if you want to. It's about having the options to plug into the industry, to learn how it works and to learn the craft. That's so important for writers to be given a fair shot.

Geoff Dyer, non-fiction writer and novelist

Let's acknowledge the help of the government in my becoming a writer. As many people of my age have said, claiming the dole used to be a recognised way of surviving in Britain. It supported a whole generation of artists, writers, dancers, musicians and so on. Those years after university, in the early 1980s, when I was reading a lot and just beginning to write, and not getting any money for it – that really wouldn't have been possible without the dole. I should also add that London was not just cheaper then, but there was also a whole economy of discounts for the unemployed, which were there to support you. It was a lovely safety net.

Now I teach creative writing in America. I've taught on these elite MFA [Master of Fine Arts] programmes in Iowa and Texas, where the students are fully funded for three or four years, and I was very conscious that the lives of the people who got onto those programmes were institutionally respectable versions of exactly the life I was living on the dole. That is to say, they're funded to spend time with a group of friends, reading and writing a lot.

Ayòbámi Adébáyò, novelist

On the computer, I have a folder where I save things that I cut or decide not to continue working on – because it's easier to feel that they might be useful at some point, rather than just throwing them away. I have at least two novels in progress in that folder, and I think I will finish them. In one instance, I didn't feel I was skilled enough to write that book yet. In a few years, I'll go back and read it, and then maybe continue, maybe not.

I've come to think of that as quite an exciting thing. I also have various projects that I've started over the years and then given up on, but I've come to think of them as glimpses of something that I might work on in the future – because I do think that work comes around. Sometimes you just aren't ready to write something.

Yes, and I also really think that everything helps. The things that have made me the writer I am are not necessarily the things that anybody has read or seen. Showing up and just working on any-thing, whether it ends up in a novel or not, is part of how I grow my sensibility as a writer – so I'm not necessarily bothered when it's clear to me that something is not going anywhere at the moment, because I think that work is always valuable in terms of my apprenticeship.

You've won places on writers' residencies over the years. I think that's a really important potential route for a writer, but it's something that not everybody thinks to apply for. Would you talk a bit about the role that those experiences had in your development?

Absolutely. I went on my first residency in 2012, and I was there for about a month. In that time, I was able to do more work on my first novel than I had done maybe in the past year, so I absolutely recommend them to anyone who's wondering if it's worth the while.

They provide two vital things. The first is the space – not just the physical space, but a mental space to focus on writing. Before my first residency, I was in university, and then I was doing an MA in literature, and for me, there was often the sense that when I was writing, I should be doing something else, whether it was studying for my exams or working on my thesis. On the residency, though, I didn't feel any pressure to do anything else.

One of the great bonuses is that often there's someone who's taking care of your meals, so you can really immerse yourself in whatever it is you're working on. Apart from that, there are usually other writers or artists in residence, so the socialising that you do is with people who are working through some of the same questions as you, or who have resolved those questions for themselves. I would work through the day and we would meet for dinner, and I could spend dinner talking about adverbs. There are very few parties or dinners that I go to where I wouldn't feel like I'm boring the other person by discussing adverbs and making a case for or against them. So these are the two vital things that residencies have provided: the time to immerse myself, and the company of other people who are also thinking and writing and creating.

Kiley Reid, novelist

Most people need to do other jobs if they want to pursue writing. When I started, I was still a nanny, and I was a receptionist for a long time, but I decided to apply to an MFA programme. The first year I applied, I didn't get in anywhere. In the second year, I did. I went to the Iowa Writers' Workshop, where everything gelled and made sense.

Iowa was the founding father of the workshop method – of bringing work in and having all of your classmates read it. Then everyone discusses your piece while you remain silent and take notes. Some sessions are terrible, and some are wonderful and you just want to run home and keep going. The opportunity to hear people talk about your work is exciting and sometimes frustrating. If your teacher isn't really engaged, or if you have a bad egg in your classroom, all of those things contribute, but I had two professors and classes that were wonderful. I workshopped my novel *Such a Fun Age* there. The best teachers always said, 'How can we make this novel the best it can be?' and I truly believe *Such a Fun Age* got better because of the workshop process.

Were there ever moments where somebody didn't like something and you disagreed with them?

Absolutely. I think that's why the numbers work out. As soon as everyone is saying, 'This chapter was confusing,' you know something has to change, but of course, there are times when you say, 'I trust my gut on this one.' Sometimes comments that you disagree with still help you identify things that need to be changed.

I had comments like, 'Why is everyone talking about money? It makes me feel really uncomfortable.' I wanted to keep that discomfort, but I decided to craft the language, pull back on the dollars and cents, and use other words that reflect people talking about money.

Did it take courage to put yourself in that environment?

It's nice to know that everyone else is a bit nervous as well – but yes, it's terrifying putting your work in front of other people, especially something that you've created recently. Most things that come with the biggest rewards take a little bit of bravery at first. For many years, I struggled with the idea of showing people my writing – but writing gets so much better when you have more eyes on it.

I had a fantastic experience, and it gave me time and space to figure out my thoughts and make a collection of work. I know I couldn't have done that when I was working fifty hours a week as a receptionist. I feel very strongly though that no one, no matter how talented they are, should go into debt trying to be a writer at one of these programmes, because it's such a financially precarious career. There are plenty of talented writers who never went anywhere near an MFA programme.

In the moment, it can seem like getting into an MFA will propel you into writing success and stability, but that's far from the truth. Even prestigious and fully funded programmes can't often fund a stable lifestyle. When I was in graduate school, I received a full tuition waiver and a $16,000 yearly stipend. That was cut down to about $13,500 when I began teaching in my second year. I had a part-time job in my first year where I made about $500 a month, and very luckily, I sold my book between my first and second year. But I did not have children, or a chronic illness, or a million other things that would have made my time in school a tenuous experience.

In the United States, you have to pay admissions fees, and for many graduate schools you have to take the GRE [Graduate Record Examinations], which you have to pay for. It's best to cast a wide net, as many fully funded programmes take only one to two per cent of applicants, but if you're applying to twelve schools and you need to take the GRE, fees will add up to around $1,000.

That vastly narrows down the pool of who can apply for an MFA, and I think this is a huge loss. Many people who have jobs and lifestyles that I'd love to see more in fiction could never afford this. So while MFA programmes can indeed advance a writer's career, I fear that they mostly advance writers of a certain income bracket, and therefore limit the material produced.

Barbara Trapido, novelist

I taught on writing courses, but I never really believed that writing could be taught. People would come along with a whole mound of writing that they clearly disliked: 'I don't like my novel, but I've got to finish it.' I tried to make people see that it wasn't compulsory – they didn't have to write a novel.

I bought some books about teaching writing, and I thought all of them were hopeless. The only one that resonated at all for me was *Taking Reality by Surprise*, a compilation, edited by Michelle Roberts, of inspiring workshop ideas that came out of a 1970s women's writing class. One required the students to write a short story in half an hour with the aid of four coloured cards, on each of which the tutor had written at random a character, a place, a dilemma and a resolution – for example, Opera Singer, Baby Clinic, Lost Briefcase, Reconciliation.

Students would do the exercise and then say, 'Oh, I love my opera singer. I'm sick of my novel – I'm going to write about the opera singer instead.' When people think they're just playing, the writing starts to get up and dance. That's what you want. You don't want it to be dead on the page. To the extent that I inspired anything, I did that.

Maggie O'Farrell, novelist

The turning point for me was when I went on a novel-writing course at the Arvon Foundation. I was taught by Elspeth Barker and Barbara Trapido.

I was about twenty-four, and I was working at the *Independent on Sunday* as a kind of desk secretary. I had about 20,000 words of what I thought was a first draft of a novel. When I think about it now, it was an absolute mess – a dog's dinner. I handed it in, and after a day or two, Elspeth and Barbara said they wanted to talk to me. I really thought, 'They've read what I've written and they think it's so terrible, they're going to ask me to leave.' I went into the room worried, thinking, 'God, it's going to be really embarrassing' – but actually they said, 'It's good, and we think you should finish it, and when you've finished it, we'll send it to our agent.'

Wow.

Yes, exactly. That was one of those moments. I still remember the absolute shock and the thrill of it. I spent the next year or so finishing it and then I sent it to their agent, Alexandra Pringle, and she was very kind to me. She said, 'You've got five plots and you can really only have one or two, and you've got far too many adverbs, and the ending doesn't work, and there's this whole supernatural strand that really isn't working' – so she told me to go away and rewrite it. I spent another year on it, because she was absolutely right about everything. At that point, she sent it out to about five publishers, and they all said no, and then I did another six months of rewrites. By this time, Alexandra was leaving to become a publisher, so Victoria Hobbs became my agent, and she remains so to this day. Victoria sent it out for submission again and it got picked up. That was what became my first book, *After You'd Gone*.

All the work was worth it. I was young and I didn't really know what I was doing – I was just feeling my way, really. The thing about novels is, you can't know where you're going. It's a bit like driving at night in the countryside without any street lights. You don't know where the turns in the road are until you're actually there, right at the last minute, when your headlights illuminate them. Writing a novel's like that. You can't think about it in the abstract. You've got to be in it, you've got to get your hands dirty – you have to be right there inside the work, in order to make it work.

Do you think you learnt a lot from that experience?

Huge amounts. It wasn't publishable at that time, and my agents were completely right to make me go back – but also, I wonder now whether they were testing if I had enough grit and determination and labour in me, because there is an awful lot of that required to write a novel. Yes, a huge amount is about inspiration and imagination, but you've also got to be a perfectionist – you've got to be able to work really hard and be very focused, and if you don't have that, you're never going to be able to finish a novel and make it work. I'd say it's probably twenty to thirty per cent inspiration and imagination, and the rest is just labour. You have to be ready for that, and you need to have the right sort of personality, and I wonder now whether it was maybe a test: 'I'll take you on as my client, but only if you are willing to put the work in' – which is fair enough.

Amer Anwar, crime writer

I'll always remember having my creative-writing MA dissertation eviscerated by my supervisor, who is a novelist. I think that was the first time anyone had really broken my writing down. You know: what's this paragraph doing? Is it conveying the information you want? Does it have the pace that you want? Does it have character? And then going down to sentence construction: is this sentence doing what you want it to? Could you combine it with another sentence to increase the pace of the book? Then down to individual word choice: could you think of a better word to convey your meaning here? I'd never really analysed it so closely, and I remember when I was later rewriting it, I had his voice in my head. 'Is this the right word? Is this sentence doing what it should? Could it be shorter?' And that really helped my writing.

Being able to take editorial feedback is very instructive, but it can be painful, don't get me wrong. You sit there, lip quivering, thinking, 'Don't cry, don't cry. It's not that bad!'

James Acaster, stand-up comic and author

At school, I was the one who played the drums and drew cartoons and was funny in drama class. I thought I was this big creative guy. Then when I was seventeen and left school, I met a bunch of people who were in a band, and they already had a record deal and had released EPs and done tours with other bands that I liked.

I only ever practised the drums during group band practice and at gigs – never on my own – but I went round to hang out with these guys, and they were all in separate rooms practising their instruments.

There are a lot of documentaries about musicians where it all feels like a fairy tale of luck and serendipity – they just got their big break and it went well for them. That's because it's really boring in a documentary to talk about practice. I remember watching the drummer of this band, who I thought was amazing, practising in his bedroom. He kept messing it up and starting again, messing it up and starting again, and I realised, 'I have to do this. I've got to work at stuff that I'm not good at, and get better at it.' Suddenly, that felt like a secret weapon.

So many adults – who, by the way, weren't doing anything creative – had told me when I was a teenager, 'Well, you need a lot of luck to succeed in those industries,' as if they knew what they were on about. I just stopped looking at it like that. There is an element of luck, but the harder you work, the less you're hanging your hopes on that. You don't have to sit back and hope that maybe one day, someone will turn to you and say, 'Do you want to write a film?'

I also realised that if I actively try to get better at something, it becomes more fun and less frustrating. I spent a day this week trying to write a screenplay that will probably never get made – but that day was really fun, and I got better as a writer while I was doing it. That's why I do this as a job, because I enjoy being creative. Even if I fail, it's a win.

Robert Webb, novelist, memoirist and comedy writer

There has been a refocusing of my career since I started writing books – but on the other hand, I still see myself as what I was originally, which was a writer-performer. David Mitchell and I wrote a lot of comedy sketches for other people at the beginning of our careers, and then we got our own radio show, and then our own TV show.

There are transferable skills from writing sketches. You learn something about economy. You learn something about painting a character very quickly with a few broad strokes. You learn not to put things in the reader's way. Alfred Hitchcock said that a confused audience doesn't emote; he was trying to scare them, whereas I'm trying to make them laugh, usually, but it's the same principle – they won't laugh if they're trying to figure something out. So some of the skills required in my writing have remained exactly the same.

Wendy Cope, poet

When kids ask me about being a poet, I say, 'You have to be good at English, or whatever language it is you want to write in.' Sometimes people think that being a poet is a spiritual condition – but you have to be good at writing, and that means being good at the school subject called English.

To what extent do you think writing is learnable?

I think that with a few pointers in the right direction, people can improve enormously, and encouragement from people you respect, who think your work is promising, will give you a huge boost.

Can you see improvement in your work, when you look back?

I've got early poems from before I was publishable, and what I can see now is that some of them read like poor imitations of Sylvia Plath, and some of them read like poor imitations of T. S. Eliot, but I didn't realise it at the time. That's a perfectly respectable journey, because it shows that at least I was reading. I think this happens to a lot of people, and I remember the first time I judged the National Poetry Competition, some of the better poems were imitations of Seamus Heaney. Now, they weren't going to win any prizes, but you thought those people might well get somewhere. If they'd got to the point of imitating Seamus Heaney, then they might work their way through to their own voice, and they would've learnt a lot.

The bad ones, the really bad ones, were people who didn't appear to have ever read anything.

André Aciman, novelist, memoirist and essayist

My father was very literary. He was a businessman, but he had read everything, and he had the habit of keeping a series of notebooks in which he would copy the sentences he liked. Imagine doing that today: copying sentences you liked, by hand! You end up walking in the shoes of the people that you're reading, which is the best training for a writer. Of course, I've never done it, so I don't know what I'm talking about.

Anna Hope, novelist

Studying creative writing helped me hugely. I did a master's degree at Birkbeck, University of London. I remember the professor at the beginning of the course saying, 'You can call yourselves writers from here on in,' and I thought, 'Whatever! We're not writers!' But actually, over time, that started to feel like a possibility.

I'm still in a fantastic group that met at Birkbeck, and carried on meeting and reading each other's work. That workshop format is a powerful experience, because you get used to critical feedback. I think it helped me hugely to believe in myself. We met weekly for, I would say, eight years, and then fortnightly for another couple of years. Now it's more like monthly, but we turn up for each other's big events. I can't really say enough about how grateful I am to that group of people. We call ourselves the Unwritables.

Everybody became much better writers, but also much better readers I think, and editors of each other's work. It was a circle of trust established over many years. I know I could ask anyone within that group to read a draft of my novel at an early stage. There are very few other people who I would feel comfortable asking to do that.

I'm published in France, and my books have been really successful there. I've realised, though, that they don't yet have such a culture of creative-writing master's degrees and workshops. It's a very American model, but in the last decade we've seen an explosion of courses in the UK. In France they don't have that attitude to craft – I think they still have the idea that a genius is just a genius.

I find it really liberating that there are so many degrees now. Of course, not everybody who does them is going to be a published writer, but at least it takes the mystique out of that. Writing is just about turning up, and sometimes the magic happens in a really potent way, but mostly it doesn't, and that's OK. Being kind to yourself through that process is hugely important; if you've got a voice on your shoulder telling you it's rubbish, that's not very kind. Over time, that voice has really quietened down for me.

David Sedaris, essayist and performer

What taught me more than anything else was a reading circuit that I got onto in Chicago. I read out loud in class at college, and then somebody in the classroom invited me to take part in a reading he was having, and gradually I started being asked to do more and more. I would often be on the bill with other people, and I learnt everything from sitting in the audience and watching them on stage.

Writers would get up there and say, 'The first of these nine poems...' and I would think, 'Fuck, we have to listen to nine poems?' All anybody wants to do is go home, and you're fooling yourself to think otherwise. Every now and then, I'll be on stage and at the end of the evening, somebody will ask me to read something specific that I've done in the past. I never do it. There's one person in the audience who wants that – the other 2,000 people don't. Sitting in an audience reminds you of everything you need to know.

Excellence teaches me a lot, and I've learnt from reading strong stylists like Joan Didion. A while ago, somebody asked me, 'What do you do when you feel like you don't have anything to write about, and you might be finished?' I said, 'I read something great.' It's like popping your eyes out and putting them in a bath and then back in your head – afterwards you think, 'OK, let's sit down and work.' Everything seems possible again.

Some people get defeated by comparing themselves to greatness. I'll go to the Met Museum with my boyfriend, who's a painter, and he'll come out saying, 'I could never paint like that.'

I don't let that kind of thought get me down. I can never be Alan Bennett, for example, but I don't feel defeated by his brilliance – I feel grateful for it. I can never be Joan Didion. I can write about people shoving things up their ass, though, and I'll get a nice laugh in Omaha. That's nothing to sneeze at.

Ruben Östlund, film-maker

There's a Swedish film-maker called Roy Andersson. I used to visit his studio in Stockholm sometimes, and on the wall, he had these small drawings that he had made with just a single dialogue line under each one. He loved to talk about them and explain them: 'Look at this. This is what I'm going to do.' He was always laughing so much while he told us about the scene, and it was such a joy for him to try to communicate what he was working on.

I think it was when I met Roy that I learnt to be open about my process, and try not to look at it always with anxiety about how hard the work is. I learnt to approach it in a joyful way: 'Look what I'm going to do!' It makes it more fun to work in this profession, and also it's a very efficient way of working: this opening up, this not shutting people out.

Mhairi McFarlane, novelist

Writing rules really upset me, because they did me a certain amount of damage when I started out. Here's a piece of bad advice I've seen: 'Don't write about any place you've never been.' That irritated me on so many levels. First of all, what nonsense when you think of a writer like George R. R. Martin! Second, it's acting as a gatekeeper against people who can't afford to be tossing off to Vienna to research a novel set there. If it feels emotionally true, then I'd rather read a good writer describing Vienna despite never having been there than a bad writer describing Vienna while sitting there at a pavement cafe.

I think some of that advice is good, and a lot of it's well meant, but it starts to attack people's judgement – and that's bad. Your judgement and your instinct are really all you have.

Looking back, was there any experience when you were starting out that particularly helped you learn?

One of the big surprises of my career was when my agent sent off the manuscript for my first novel to a professional service run by a woman called Joanna Rees. They don't take on a manuscript that they don't think has potential; you pay a fee, and they give you a report on how to make it saleable. Joanna came back and she basically taught me how to write a book.

I was absolutely knee-knocking when I opened that report, but she was so positive and so kind. It's embarrassing to admit, but she taught me unbelievably basic things, like to vary where my scenes are set; don't keep taking the reader back to the same flat or same house – give them new places. She cut a lot of the verbiage.

She also told me something amazing, which I didn't think was true at the time. She said, 'The hardest thing you will ever have to do in a story is work out how you put all the people who need to be in a room into that room.' At the time, I thought, 'What a load of nonsense! You're the god of that universe. Of course you can put people into a room' – but it's really true. The next time you see a film, you'll realise how many times they have to contrive situations so that the right people can talk to each other. These things seem effortless when they're done right. When they're done badly, they really clank.

Brandon Taylor, novelist

I applied to the Iowa Writers' Workshop because I wanted an education. I felt like I had been trying to figure out how to be a writer and what writing was by myself, and I was lost in the wilderness. I wanted to find a place to be among other people who cared as much as I did about words.

I don't think I actually learnt anything technical in the classroom – but it was the best place for me to be at that time. I had already written my debut novel *Real Life*, and when I finished that, I didn't write fiction for five months. I felt like I had used up everything. I didn't know to have faith that I would write again.

In Iowa, I was surrounded by all of these people who had written books and who were still writing, and it gave me hope – and because I was in a writing programme, I had to produce material to workshop for class. It was like the place was goading me to get back to work, and what my teachers gave me was the sense that the most important thing is the work. Validation is nice, but it is subordinate to the work – and what you must do, when you finish a story, is turn the page and begin again.

Craig Taylor, non-fiction writer, playwright and editor

One of the most depressing things about working as an editor is you see just how many people out there want to express themselves and be seen and write, but they don't really want to read. They're not interested, and that just shines through.

There has to be a real promiscuity with reading. To read all over the place is so necessary, so it's not just the books that are being published right now, or the books that have been well-reviewed – you're going back in time, you're switching gender, you're going as far as you possibly can.

What do you find most difficult about writing?

It's a never-ending struggle to write a proper sentence, to be grammatically correct, to understand how language fits together. I struggle with every single level, from the word choice to the sentence, to the way to form a paragraph, to the larger themes – but I think it's great to fail at writing again and again. Practise low-level failure your entire life, so that you don't become pompous – which destroys writers and their relevance to the world – and you always know that there's this mystery beyond you that you'll never get to solve, and something you can work at but will never truly master.

I think it's a wonderful reason to keep doing it every day – this sense of purposeful failure. 'Try again. Fail again. Fail better,' as Beckett said. I love that idea. I just love it.

9

What's so hard about being read?

'I think a lot of writers are extremely sensitive.
You have to be, to let the world in.'

ELIZABETH DAY, novelist, journalist and non-fiction writer

A week before I released the first season of the *In Writing* podcast, I dreamt that I was at an unfamiliar table in a walled courtyard. There was a meal in front of me, and I was doing my best with it, but it was hard to act normal because also around the long dining table was a firing squad with rifles trained at my head. If my subconscious is a storyteller, it's the type that prizes dramatic symbolism over narrative nuance. I had convinced myself that in releasing the podcast, I was risking professional death.

I had spent six months quietly recording and editing it, and although my confidence had fluctuated all along, it was only now that I was really losing my mind. The potential consequences of releasing a dud started to loom large. I imagined my journalism work drying up, and whispered conversations between my peers: 'Have you listened to Hattie's podcast? My god . . . how embarrassing.'

I called my sister in a panic, and she reassured me in a slow, puzzled way, as you would speak to someone who's taken too many drugs and thinks the table lamp is giving them a hateful look.

I had become terrified, and with it, I'd fallen down an ego hole: I not only thought that my project was bad, but also that everyone was going to be deeply interested in how bad it was.

It was too late to go back – I'd interviewed too many people with the promise that there was a podcast coming – so I released it anyway. People listened to it, and they were kind, and I did not die. I now recognise this madness as the last stage of my personal creative process, because as I approached the end of this book, I heard rifles being loaded, and a persistent voice shouting, 'What if it's terrible?'

Eventually, your work has to leave you. It has to go to teachers, agents, editors, booksellers, production companies, readers, critics and maybe even award judges; it might be read by your parents, your partner, and a neighbour who will soon know a hell of a lot more about you than you do about them. It's hard to let go of a precious, private project in which you've invested so much. It feels like taking your clothes off outside the town hall and asking passers-by to rate and review.

This chapter is about exactly that leap from private to public. The people I've interviewed here have all written professionally; they have drummed up the courage to send out their work time and again, and many of them have good advice on how to manage the anxiety. They've faced all of our fears: some have received painful rejections, where others have had to swallow negative press or engage with trolls. They've laboured over books that failed to be published, and in more than one case, they've published books that they wish they hadn't.

In other words, when a writer sends out their work, difficult things might happen. Critical feedback is the main one that's unavoidable, and ultimately often good for us. My root-canal surgery was also unavoidable and good for me, but that doesn't mean I was jazzed about it.

After many years in journalism, I've just about mastered the appropriate gracious response to editorial notes: take a few deep breaths. Express gratitude for the help, even if you want to push the person who offered the help into a river, and even if you hate all their suggestions and believe them to be moronic. Remember that your mother loves you. Remember that you've survived much worse than this. Remember that the critique is only of something you've made, but how you address it will tell you something about who you are.

For all the terror I felt about sharing the podcast, my life is unequivocally better for having done so. Maybe the anxiety it induced was proportionate to its potential to change my life, because it really did: it was a step onto a different creative path, which has given me a huge amount of pleasure. It's rewarding to share something you've made and to talk to other people about it, and as we saw in the previous chapter, it teaches you a lot.

Although some of the experiences here might fill the aspiring writer with dread, the important point is that everyone survived and kept on writing. It's helpful, if you're going to press ahead, to identify people who will support you and cheerlead when necessary. I recently confided my nerves to my old friend Nat, who works as a barrister. He sent me a long and kind message in response, reminding me that we all doubt ourselves. 'Often, just before I give a speech in court, I have a paralysing thought: what gives me the right to do this?' he wrote. 'There are all sorts of good and legitimate answers to that question, but increasingly the one that helps me recover composure is this: fuck it! Life's too short.'

It wouldn't fly in court, but it works for me. Life *is* short. If you love to write, be brave and let them read it.

Anna Hope, novelist

The experience of writing my first book was joyous, and with it I got my wonderful agent, whom I still have today. I was really interested in the Victorian spiritualist movement and how working-class women had emancipated themselves through holding seances. It was such a strange little pocket of history, and I'd yoked it to a suffragette story. The elements didn't quite marry up. There was a really lovely editor who was interested in buying it, but she wasn't able to convince enough of her team.

That was really hard. In retrospect, I can see what was wrong with it, but at the time I was living in it and it was pretty devastating. I considered giving up on writing, and training as a teacher, but a little while later I had an idea for another novel. My husband gave me a month to be sad, and then one day he woke me up with a coffee in my Virginia Woolf *Room of One's Own* mug, and he said, 'Get up. Write another book.'

He'd seen how dedicated I'd become to my writing practice and he also, amazingly, said that he would pay the rent on our little flat. That meant that I could cut the number of shifts I was doing in a call centre and just concentrate on writing in the morning, and that carried on through the time that I wrote my next book, *Wake*.

That was not an easy process either. I wrote draft after draft that didn't work, and my agent, who is phenomenally rigorous and brilliantly insightful, would read them and say, 'Hmm, there's something that's still not working.' It was right to the wire with that book. One day, she phoned me and said, 'It's ready to go out.'

How exciting – but also how nerve-wracking, after what you'd been through with the first one.

It was – the stakes were high. It went out on a Tuesday, and I remember working in the call centre and seeing a call from her. I went into the breakout room and answered, and she said, 'There's a pre-empt from a publisher, but it looks like it's going to auction.' There was a seven-way auction, and my life changed.

Kit de Waal, novelist and short-story writer

The first novel I wrote never even got sent to publishers, because my agent at the time said it wasn't very good, and she was right. One of the criticisms was that there were too many characters. At a very critical juncture, my protagonist goes into a bagel shop in London, because it's the middle of the night and he's hungry and he's just committed a terrible crime. This Chinese guy is serving him the bagel, and then I'm off. I'm off with the Chinese guy's mum. Who is she? Where does she live? Oh, she's disabled, she's upstairs.

Nobody wants to know! I did that so many times in the novel, it's embarrassing to think about. To me, the Chinese guy's really interesting – but we're trying to follow the protagonist, so just stop it.

The second one did go to publishers, and the publishers didn't want it – and that was terrible. It was extremely depressing to have somebody say, 'Oh, this isn't very good.' They said it was too literary to be a thriller and too much of a thriller to be literary. I'd spent years on it, I loved it, but it just didn't work.

It was a nightmare and I did not take it in good grace. I didn't immediately say, 'Fine, I'll write another one' – I was bereft. I thought, 'OK, my literary life will be short stories. I know I can do that, and I'll just stick to that.' Then after six months or so, I decided to write my novel *My Name Is Leon*. I was fifty-five years old when I sold it, and fifty-six when it came out.

Meg Mason, novelist

My first published book was a memoir and I wish that I could take it back. It feels like my teenage diary, because I wrote it without any wisdom or understanding. As a magazine writer, which is what I was at the time, you only have a sense of your work being really temporal – but when it's a book, it will be around forever. It's like getting a tattoo on your face.

It was about my experiences of being a young and not madly happy mother, and I didn't understand what the impact of that would be. I wrote without a view to anything beyond the writing and I hadn't really resolved all my tricky feelings. People say, 'Don't drive angry' – I was writing angry, and it comes through.

I read it recently for the first time in a really long time and I was horrified. I couldn't recognise that person at all. I got really upset and I said to my husband, 'Was I really so awful?' He said, 'Everybody was awful ten years ago, but none of us wrote it down.' It was such a kind thing to say but I still struggle with the book's existence.

David Nicholls, novelist and screenwriter

In my twenties I tried to be an actor, and that didn't work out, and then I had some success writing for TV. I really enjoyed it and I wrote some episodes of the show *Cold Feet*, which did well.

I developed a couple of other things with different TV companies, and they were green-lit, which is the writer's dream.

One was a show called *Rescue Me* about magazine journalists. This was about the time of *Sex and the City*, and I'd written a very melancholy show about divorce and misery and loneliness in London, and it didn't do very well. We really put heart and soul into it, and it just didn't get the audiences. It was too metropolitan or . . . well, probably not well written enough. It didn't get a second series, and so suddenly I didn't have any work. I didn't have anything to write. I wasn't being asked to do anything. The time I'd put aside to write the second series was empty.

I'd always wanted to write about university and yet there was a rule in British television: no shows about students. The general audience don't care if the essay doesn't get done; they don't care if the characters are drunk all the time. I was always trying to pitch university shows and they never went anywhere. So I was just jotting down ideas in first-person prose, and I thought, 'Well, maybe it's a monologue.' Then I wrote a longer section, and I thought that maybe it had potential as a comic novel. I gave it to a friend of mine and said, 'What do you think of this?' She passed it to an agent, and the agent liked it, and that became my first book, *Starter for Ten*.

Often the steps you take professionally don't come out of success – they come out of failure. If I'd done at all well as an actor, even if I'd had a very small break, I'd have kept on acting. If I'd had a more consistent career as a screenwriter, I'd have kept on screenwriting. In both professions I came to a dead end, and that's when I took up the next thing – which isn't to say it was a concession. I just didn't have the confidence to write a novel, until I was forced to.

Mhairi McFarlane, novelist

I left my journalism job at the *Nottingham Post* in 2007, and I was already well on the way to having written my first novel, *You Had Me at Hello* – but it wasn't published until 2012. It was 'maturing in wood', sitting in a drawer, for five years before it came out.

Why was that?

I left the *Post* with a combination of arrogance, stupidity and optimism, thinking, 'Well, I'm a journalist – I know how to write clean copy. The industry will be waiting for me and my take on the chick-lit novel.' I thought that I would be published within two years. Of course, the industry isn't waiting for you, and finding an agent's really hard, and you get loads of knock-backs. People are always asking me for writing advice, but to be honest, the most useful thing I can say to anybody is: don't be stupid like I was and give up your full-time job, thinking, 'I've got a real winner on my hands with this manuscript.' You just don't know.

I got my agent in 2009, and she commissioned a rewrite of the novel, which was really good and kicked it into shape. Then we started shopping it around, but it was a tricky time for a romantic comedy. It was a long time after *Bridget Jones*, which started the gold rush for women's commercial fiction in that vein. It was felt that the genre had become stale and tired. Something I've learnt about publishing is you're probably better off trying to sell quite a weak book in the hot genre than something well-written in a genre that they're currently uninterested in.

When HarperCollins eventually picked it up in 2012, every other women's fiction department had already said no – and I was pretty low, it must be said. It was a very modest advance they gave me, which was absolutely fair enough, because I wasn't tried and tested.

When you pull back the velvet curtain, writers all have stories like this. Things can look easy or effortless, and the real story can be knottier or more complicated, and involve a lot more rejections. That's useful to know, because rejections are so tough.

Jon Ronson, storyteller and author

When I was twenty, I wrote a radio play and sent it to the BBC. I'm not exaggerating when I say that this was their reply: 'We can't offer you encouragement. You have no idea what you're doing.'

Kiley Reid, novelist

Rejections are not easy, and, oh my goodness, I had more than I could count. The first nine graduate-school rejections, all in one year – that was rough. You think, 'Maybe this isn't for me.' I had so many short-story rejections too, and then there were days where I got a good one – 'This isn't right, but try us again,' or 'This almost made it' – and then you live off that one sentence for the next four months. I'm proud of going past the rejections and of not submitting the same stories again without changes. I'm proud of taking the feedback I've had and changing the work into something I can stand by.

Amer Anwar, crime writer

Long before it was published, the first chapter of my first novel won the Crime Writers' Association's Debut Dagger award. I had a great agent and a great editor, both of whom were really excited about the book, so I felt confident that it would get picked up. When it was ready, my agent sent it out to all the big publishing houses, all the crime imprints, and it got rejected by every single one.

To get all those rejections after eight years of putting in a lot of work on the manuscript was quite heartbreaking. The feedback that I got from publishers was confusing, because it was all really positive. They were saying it had great characters, setting, plot, action, dialogue, and yet they were still saying, 'I just don't think we can publish it. We don't have the right mission plan. It doesn't quite fit our list.' I was scratching my head thinking, 'Well, what more do you want in a crime thriller? It's ticking all the boxes.' Then with one comment, the penny dropped. Somebody said, 'I can't visualise it breaking out to a broad audience.'

Right. What they were getting at is that your novel is set in a British Asian community, and they weren't sure white people would read it.

Reading between the lines, that was exactly it. Nobody could come out and say, 'Well, it's a bit too Asian' – how would that sound?

It's set in Southall, west London. There are a lot of Asian references, there's a bit of Punjabi language. But I'd been very conscious writing that book: first and foremost, it was a crime thriller for anybody who likes crime thrillers – it just happened that those characters are from that background. It's like when you're cooking something and you add a bit of spice to lift it, or that's what I thought.

I decided to self-publish, and I wanted to give it the best possible chance. I spent six months on social media watching how the big publishers launch their books. I designed adverts and little posts for Twitter and Facebook. I took photographs in Southall and designed my own cover. I even set up a fake publisher – there's a logo on the spine, so that when it's on a bookshelf, it looks legit, and when you open it up, it's got a copyright page. I learnt how to typeset the book, got an ISBN number, did the barcode myself – it all looks very professional. One of my old bosses has a print company and he printed my proof copies for free. I saw that publishers would send bloggers their books to generate buzz, so I did the same. I wrote my own press release, pretending to be my publicist. I had email addresses and signatures that said 'publicity department'.

I can see now how you come up with your crime thriller plots. You're a cunning man.

I went to every bookshop that I could get to. I'd show the manager a copy of my book and they would order a few. I realised that cities like Birmingham, Leicester and Coventry also have big Asian communities, so I emailed bookshops there to see if they'd be interested in stocking a British Asian thriller. It started to be sold around the country, and I started to get Amazon reviews and emails from readers. One of the reviews said, 'I don't think I'm the target audience for this book, because I'm white, female, over forty and Scottish – but I absolutely loved it.' I thought, 'Yes! That's exactly who I want to enjoy the book.'

I'd go to festivals and events and tout the book around, and eventually I was introduced to Sharmaine Lovegrove, who had just set up Dialogue Books with Little, Brown. I told her about my book, and I sent it to her on a Thursday. On Monday, I got a phone call: 'Could you come in for a meeting?'

Dialogue eventually republished it, and *The Times* and the

Guardian listed it as one of their thrillers of the year. It was a phenomenal feeling.

Your experience shows that writers of colour are not always getting the opportunities that they deserve.

I think that's very much the case with some publishers. Writers are turned down if the characters don't behave in ways that the publisher imagines of people from those backgrounds. I think if someone has no experience of mixing with people from other backgrounds, then they feel uncomfortable – yet readers are the sort of people who can live outside of their own experience, and appreciate that, and have greater empathy, so I honestly can't explain it. I guess it's what they call unconscious bias – or maybe conscious, in some people's cases.

Grace Dent, restaurant critic, YA writer and memoirist

Some people just don't get you. If you're working as a freelance writer, and an editor commissions you to write a 600-word piece but they give you a 350-word brief, and when you file the copy they send back six questions – unless you're the worst writer in the world, it's likely that this place just isn't for you.

I've worked everywhere, and I've met four or five editors in my life who just get me. They say, 'Grace, we need a piece on this,' and I write it, and it may be cluttered and it may be full of spelling mistakes, but they look at it and go, 'Right, I get that. And yes, we're going to keep that joke in, even though it's really niche, because that's Grace.' You need to find people who believe in you and your writing.

John Lanchester, novelist and non-fiction writer

What is appealing at the beginning of writing a book is the thought of how great it's going to be when you look back on it, and it's worked.

Yes, and it's actually quite hard to locate that moment. You finish writing a book, and is that the great moment? Or is it when the first person reads it and likes it? Or is it the moment when an agent or an editor takes it on, or is it when you've responded to the editorial notes, or is it when you get the proofs, or is it when you finish with the proofs and send them back, or is it when you have the first copy in your hands and you're waiting for it to actually come out? You have to work out for yourself when you get that moment of 'Oh, it's done.'

What I observe in friends who've written books is that actually it's a much more anxious process than they anticipated, and even when the book comes out, they're waiting to see whether it'll be reviewed and what the reviews will be like. I wonder whether you have to let the dust settle and then look back on it with satisfaction. What's it like for you?

It is anxious. I wish I could tell you I've solved all that, but I'm not sure I have. I try to like the moment when I feel I've finished it, and the bit when I hand it over to my wife as my first reader. That's when I try to collect myself around the fact that it's done, because even if you get knocked down by a bus, or if everybody hates it, there's still that thing of its doneness.

I think the anxiety is linked to the fact that it's not a clear-cut thing, having a book out. I often feel envy of people in the arts who have something like a first night – you know, your play opens, or the gallery opens, or your concert happens, and that's the thing. The whole thing about writing and reading is that it's to do with absence. You're not there when the audience is reacting, and almost by definition, writers are people who like not being there. The type of person who is all about presence and direct engagement with people isn't usually a writer. Writers are people who like to process things privately and internally, and in a sense be somewhere else when the reaction is happening. That does mean there's a weirdness and a displacement.

That was one of Kingsley Amis's theories about why so many writers are drunks – it's a displaced stage fright. Instead of getting stage fright for the first night like an actor, for writers it's happening all the time. Somebody could be reading your book right now. Right at this moment, somebody could be completely hating your work.

Liane Moriarty, novelist

I saw one review where they used the term 'baggy' for my novels.

You read your reviews, then?

I've put on the public record that I don't, but now I've outed myself, because I know that word: 'baggy'. I do not read Amazon reviews or Goodreads reviews, but sometimes I've seen a headline and it seems like it's positive, so I've thought, 'Oh, I might be safe to go into that one.' Then I think, 'Oh no, you shouldn't have' – because there are some nice paragraphs, but the only thing I can remember of it is the word 'baggy'.

I saw the other day that someone had written a really bad review on social media and then tagged the author in it to make sure she would see it. I don't understand the rationale of that.

It's such bad manners. Sometimes people put reviews on my own Facebook page – and I think, 'Surely it's safe – they wouldn't have put it here otherwise.' Often it is mostly positive, but of course the only thing you remember is the negative thing. Then sometimes well-meaning friends want to tell you about something negative that they've read, that they disagree with, or that somebody else disagreed with. You don't need to tell me!

You have two sisters who are published authors. Is it helpful to be able to talk to them about this stuff?

Yes, I do feel very lucky that we're there for each other. If I accidentally happen upon the description of my plots as baggy, I can text my sisters and they can say, 'What are they talking about? That's the most ridiculous thing I've ever heard.' All of us are very good at outrage on each other's behalf.

Emily St. John Mandel, novelist and screenwriter

This is approximately the least sympathetic problem in the world, but if you've had a very successful novel, there is a fear: 'Will anybody like the new book as much as they liked my previous book?'

The publication process can be hard. You pour your heart and soul into a book for years so that somebody on Twitter can go, 'Nah.' It's hard when there are bad reviews that fundamentally mistake something that happened in the book: you can't really respond to them without seeming insane, but sometimes they'll be based on a problem that just isn't there. They'll say, 'Mandel never explained X,' but I did explain X, for three chapters. That can be frustrating.

Awards can also be a little bit deranging. There's a Hilary

Mantel quote that I had written on an index card on my wall for a long time. She said, 'I'm glad I was a Booker judge relatively early in my career. It stopped me thinking that literary prizes are about literary value.' I've looked at that every award season. When you have a book that didn't make the long list or the short list or win the prize, it's helpful to remember that it is just the opinion of five people, or however big the judging panel is. It's just the titles that all the judges could agree on – it's not really about who's better or worse. I try to remember that anyway, because of course, I'd like to win all the awards.

David Sedaris, essayist and performer

What's interesting now is that in publishing, everyone's been through all of the training they have to attend at the office, and they are so convinced that certain things just aren't funny any more, because it's nothing they could get away with saying at work. The truth is, the same things are funny that have always been funny, and an audience roars with laughter at them.

My agent came to me a while ago and said, 'Gosh, I'm so sorry. The *New Yorker* just turned that essay down.' I said, 'It includes setting homeless people on fire and cooking your food over the flames. Of course they weren't going to publish it.' If you said to my audience, 'Do you think it's OK to make jokes about homeless people?' they would say, 'No, absolutely not.' If you said, 'Do you think it's OK to consider lighting them on fire?' they would say, 'No, that's horrible.' But I read the essay to them on tour and they roar with laughter.

It must be the way you tell them.

It's partly because it's not expected, and it's partly because of the way it builds – but also, I'm not serious. I'm not suggesting that anybody go out there and set anybody on fire, and everybody knows that. But a magazine has to be afraid that somebody's going to take it out of context and tweet about it, and blah, blah, blah.

I get my fair amount of outraged mail, and I have to say, I don't give a fuck. I really don't give a fuck!

Will Storr, long-form journalist and author

What have you found most challenging over your years as a writer?

The first thing is making a living. That's been really tough. Being a freelance journalist was hard, and I was doing that a few years ago – now I don't know how people manage, especially as they get into middle age and they've got mortgages and other responsibilities.

Then failure is one of the hardest things to deal with. As any creative person, you are constantly dealing with failure, whether it's a draft of a piece that gets sent back three times – or god forbid, spiked – or it's a draft of a book and you get voluminous notes from an obviously unimpressed editor. It never gets easier.

The thing I hate most about the process is getting reviews, because you've got this dichotomy: you really want them, because it means you're relevant and you might sell some books, but getting reviews is awful. You're being judged by peers and sometimes people who are above you, so it's like getting your exam results. It's completely humiliating if they don't like it, because everybody that you know and value and love is going to read that review – and you're so angry. You're never far from failure as a writer. I think that's the hardest thing.

I agree. As a freelance journalist, I've had moments over the years of thinking, 'Why did I choose to throw myself into a career where I'm constantly reminded of my relative success or failure?' And you can flip so quickly between those two as well. You can have a run of a few good weeks or months where lots of things are being published, and money's coming in very smoothly – and then you can have an article that the editor just hates, and keeps sending back to you, and then you can have three weeks where you don't have any work. My opinion of myself, how I rate myself – it's up and down like a yo-yo, thanks to my job.

One of the maddening psychological effects is that if you get a bad review, or you get an article sent back, it's as if every achievement that you have had as a writer means nothing. The fact is, you're a crap writer. You're useless. You should just give up and open a sandwich shop.

Nothing that's gone before matters.

It doesn't matter. It was all a lie, and this is the truth. I'm forty-five now and I still get that feeling acutely, for days, so it never goes away, and because of the online thing it's now much, much worse for journalists. When I was writing at the *Guardian*, they brought in the comments section. It's horrific, because you're expected to engage with the commenters, and of course, it's completely toxic in there. It always used to amaze me that the *Guardian* would see themselves as having such a liberal, kindly worldview, and yet they would expect their members of staff to engage in ritual abuse with every piece written.

I once wrote a piece about how lonely I was, and my wife said, 'Oh, the comments are good this time.' So I looked at them. There was one guy who'd said, 'I've never read such narcissism. This person is completely self-obsessed,' and so on – it was an unbelievably personal attack. Somebody else had written, 'Well I feel sorry for Will if he's reading this,' and then the first guy had come back and said, 'I don't.'

I thought, 'I'm never reading the comments again.' It was really upsetting. When it's confessional stuff, you're exposing your soul – and people are going, 'Well, I've seen your soul, and my conclusion is that you're an arsehole.'

It is brutal. It really is.

Elizabeth Day, novelist, journalist and non-fiction writer

I really don't like to show work in progress to other authors, or to friends. When you criticise me, you have to be quite careful in how you express it, because I am really quite thin-skinned. I've worked hard on that, and I try not to be, but I think a lot of writers are extremely sensitive. You have to be, to let the world in.

Cressida Cowell, children's writer and illustrator

I've learnt not to be afraid of being emotional in my work, though of course that makes me vulnerable. In the end, not everybody is going to love what I write, but I think it's better to write something that is moving, and that resonates for some people, even if others think it's a bit silly. I'd rather fail in flames than not try. You've got to be able to make mistakes, and not be afraid of going out into unknown territory and making a fool of yourself – because you've only got one life.

Graham Norton, novelist

The public have known you for so many years as a comedian and chat-show host. Did you have any anxiety, when your first novel came out, about asking them to see you in a slightly different way?

I remember thinking, 'I haven't done this before. I'm trying. The publishers have gone ahead with it, and they're claiming it's going to be in shops.' Then I had to brace myself: 'OK, what's the worst-case scenario? It becomes the joke *du jour*, and everybody laughs about how bad Graham Norton's novel was.'

But that would be awful. Weren't you dreading that possibility?

I was, but you gird your loins for it. 'OK, that's the worst thing that can happen, and then I go back to my day job. I allow my friends to enjoy my humiliation, but the vast majority of the people who watch my show on BBC One won't know I've written a book.' You have to put it in some sort of perspective: yes, it would have embarrassed me personally and hurt me emotionally, but it wouldn't have damaged my main career. It wasn't like I'd walked out of the TV studios going, 'That's it! I'm a writer. I'm wearing corduroy and nothing else. Respect me.' I wasn't doing that. I was going, 'Look, here's this little book.' I wasn't overreaching myself, writing some sort of state-of-the-nation tome. It wasn't a family saga covering hundreds of years, or a history of the famine. It was very small in scope, so I made it as safe as I could for myself.

In a way, I think that fear made it a better book. If I'd had no name, I think my first attempt would have been much more ambitious and florid and overwritten. I kept metaphors to a minimum, because I was afraid of people saying, 'Why is Graham Norton comparing this to that?'

Mona Arshi, poet, novelist and essayist

I wrote a poem called 'Bad Day in the Office', and I never thought about it being about postnatal depression, but that's how it was critically received. Audiences talk about it, readers respond to it in that way, and in fact the reader is much wiser than the poet. Maybe I had blind spots about the poem, and they were the better judges of its meaning. I let go, and I accept it – it's no longer my business.

Zoe Williams, journalist

You've published two books – but the way you talk about them, I get the impression that you don't feel they were successes.

Oh no, they were terrible failures. One was a book about contemporary British politics called *Get It Together* – it had the shortest window of relevance of any book I've ever encountered. There were bits of it that I stand by, and I think are even more relevant now than they were in 2015, for example, about the housing crisis. But nobody's going back to 2015 to find out what I think about the housing crisis now. It completely missed its mark.

Perhaps some of the responsibility for that lies with the publisher, though.

Yeah, maybe. Well, they paid for it, and they sure as hell didn't get their money back.

Lucy Prebble, playwright and screenwriter

You wrote two series of the TV show Secret Diary of a Call Girl, *which were hugely popular – but then you chose to leave. Anyone*

from the outside would have seen that job as a success, but to you
as a writer, it didn't feel right. Why was that?

I'm surprised that I did leave. It's hard to connect to that person
completely. I was very much an employee of people who thought
they had a good machine – which was a show with a recognisable
actress in it, Billie Piper, about a rather salacious and interesting
world. The channel was really interested in it being lightweight. I
didn't like the show that I was making, and at some point I had to
work out whether I was going to change the show so that I liked
it, or not work on the show that I didn't like. There wasn't really a
third option for me.

At the time, to be really honest, I felt I'd failed people and let
them down, and was cowardly for not going on with it. I felt very
bad about it. Now when I look back, what I feel I learnt was that I
wouldn't be happy in a situation where I was an employee trying
to meet a vision I didn't believe in. Also, maybe on a more controlling level, I realised that I didn't want to be the sort of writer
who wrote scripts, delivered them, then didn't really care what
happened after that. That was not a particularly happy set-up for
me, and now I wouldn't be in one like that.

Wendy Cope, poet

My first book sold very well, and that was a mixed blessing. It
made me very unpopular with some poets, and I've had a rather
difficult relationship with the poetry world ever since.

Then my second book got a really terrible review in the *TLS*,
and that mattered because it was the only thing that was seen
abroad, and it was completely unfair. It was obviously because my
first book had done so well and the critic thought he'd tear me

down. I've bumped into him a couple of times at parties and said, 'Oh, sorry, I don't speak to you,' and walked away. He's the only person I will do that to, because I was so cross about that review.

There are different kinds of reviews. The best ones are good reviews by people who have really understood. Then there are nice reviews, full of praise, by people who really haven't got the point at all, but that's better than being nasty. What I want is intelligent reviews; I don't mind if it's an intelligent review with a few negative things in it. Then you get really spiteful reviews, like that one.

I've got lots of friends now who are poets, and some of them once thought I was terrible. It helps when you get to know them. At one time, I'd be introduced to some poet I'd never met, and they'd look at me as if they were being asked to shake hands with Hitler. There really was a huge amount of prejudice against me.

What do you think that was really about?

It's very difficult for poets when their books aren't selling much and they haven't got many readers, and then someone pops up and does very well. When somebody comes along who's popular, there's always the consoling idea that they're no good. You know, there are these Instagram poets at the moment – they're no good and they're terribly popular, and I find it very annoying.

Curtis Sittenfeld, novelist

If your work is terrible, or if you think it's good but it doesn't sell, I think you still can learn a lot. It can be an exercise of completing a big project that's useful and satisfying. Maybe you've taught yourself to write a novel, and next time you can teach yourself to write a good novel.

In all honesty, I don't stand by my second book, *The Man of My Dreams* – some people, not by accident, don't know it exists. I think it's fine at the level of the sentence, but I don't think it's well structured, and I learnt a really important lesson early on from that, which is that I can't control anything about the process except whether or not I put a book into the world that I stand by and feel proud of.

Ever since then, I've had fluctuating sales, fluctuating reviews, but all the books I've published are books that I would like to read. And in the end, how else do you assess quality, or worthwhileness, or justification for how you spend your own time?

Geoff Dyer, non-fiction writer and novelist

In the film world, there's a tradition that somebody makes a number of stupid superhero films, and then on the basis of that, they become bankable enough to do their 'passion project'. The passion project, of course, often turns out to be every bit as stupid as the superhero films. So that's the model, if you like – you gain an economic base, and then you go on to do your individual thing.

I think as often as not, though, that doesn't work, because for all sorts of reasons you become dependent on those big-money projects. I've found that I've been able to achieve a measure of independence – or so I've convinced myself – by virtue of a history not of success, but of failure, whereby because my previous books had sold so badly and there was such a small audience for them that nobody gave a toss whether I did more of the same at a very low level, or did something at a similarly low level that was completely different. Weirdly, then, I've had this freedom that is born out of not having an audience. I've been able to do different things, really quite selfishly, with only one person in mind – namely, me.

Do you care about reviews?

In a typical narcissistic way, I'm always in the market for praise. I start reading a review thinking, 'Oh, this will be nice. I'll get a nice stroke here.' Then I realise, 'Oh my god, it's not a stroke. I'm on the receiving end of a headbutt, and my nose is streaming blood.' So yeah, I don't like that at all.

With my last book, I was surprised not just by the fact that people didn't like the book, but by how vehemently they came out against it. You could say that the author is necessarily blind to the faults that are so obvious to the reader. Well, that's one way of looking at it. But my sense of the book was entirely unaltered by all of the adverse comments about it. My good opinion of it emerged unscathed.

I'm really glad to hear that.

Actually, Hattie, unlike Thomas Hardy – who famously said that the response to *Jude the Obscure* cured him of further interest in novel writing – I emerged feeling more confident than ever as a result of the stick that I'd taken.

10

What are the writer's rewards?

'What matters is, do you really love the art of storytelling?'

ELIF SHAFAK, novelist

The last time I interviewed George Saunders, he wished me good luck with this book and offered an observation about the creative-writing community, whom he knows well thanks to his online Story Club. 'It's amazing how many people are interested in this craft now, and even making it the linchpin of their lives,' he said. 'There's almost a spiritual component.'

George knows what he's talking about. Since 1997, long before he gathered an audience of hundreds of thousands online, he's been teaching writing at Syracuse University; he also wrote a wonderful book dissecting the Russian short story, *A Swim in a Pond in the Rain*. He sees the process with clarity, articulates it in reassuringly ordinary language, and encourages us to work at it gently and with patience. He believes there's something magical in how a story evolves – but he doesn't make it sound so mysterious that it's out of reach.

I'll listen to anything he has to say on the matter, which is why his comment lingered. So many things about writing professionally are challenging, and yet I chose to do it, and I continue to choose it wholeheartedly. Why? Is it spiritual?

One reason is that writing brings me comfort. I escape the world and go inwards, to somewhere dark, soft and silent. That's how it feels in deep concentration, and it's why if somebody arrives unexpectedly and I have to switch into social mode, I am clunky and bewildered for a while, trying to remember how to be normal. Left alone, I can summon an illusion of control: I can consider the human experience, and by organising it into sentences and paragraphs, I can soothe myself that life is manageable.

Then there's the fact that being a writer is a lifelong project that brings the satisfaction of progress. I think writers write not only despite how difficult it is, but because it's difficult. What goes on in that safe, nest-like place is always a wrestling match, with ideas and feelings robustly resisting my efforts to express them, but I grapple and I gain ground eventually; I find that I like myself more along the way, because I'm proud that I persist. One of the deepest rewards of writing, but also of talking and thinking about it for so many years, has been a shift in my perspective: for a long time, I believed the struggles that I had as a writer to be a sign of my inadequacy, and I saw the struggles that I had as a human in the same light. Now, I think that writing is both hard and wonderful, and that life too is hard and wonderful, and that we make them meaningful by continuing to try.

Third, I write to understand and connect with others. I love it when I'm interviewing someone, and they are searching for the right word, and I can supply it. There is no better response from an interviewee than 'Exactly,' because in that instant, we share the unshareable: what it's like to be us. In writing, I try to transmit as honestly and specifically as possible my perceptions – about the person I've interviewed, or about this craft, or about the twelve best skirts for autumn/winter – so that the reader, whether they agree or not, can for a moment feel them too. We're both engaged in empathy, which I think is a faculty worth strengthening. Several writers in this chapter explain that their connection with readers motivates them more than any other part of the job.

My work, then, helps me to make sense of the world and my beliefs and values within it; it's a continuing practice that both challenges me and keeps me sane, and it's an act of love for others. Considered like that, maybe it is spiritual.

There are other motivations to pick up a pen too – rewards that are less lofty but equally attractive. 'I do like the attention,' confesses journalist Zoe Williams, and she's far from the only one – my own ego flashes like a lighthouse when someone responds to my work. There are many juicier things that writers expect to be validating: wild sales figures; stories being adapted for Hollywood; awards stacking up. What's it like when those dreams come true? In this chapter, successful writers spill some complicated beans.

There's one last, trivial thing that I'll admit to fantasising about since long before I started on a book: a launch party. Give me time to get out of my brain-nest, and I can be very sociable. When I interviewed former *Vogue* editor Alexandra Shulman, she said, 'I think journalists in particular, but often authors and poets and biographers and all kinds of writers, are the best company. The best parties are journalists' parties, because there is that hunger for the exchange of information, and that interest in what other people say.' I don't exactly write for party invitations, but I almost always accept them when they come.

Writers – introspective, entertaining, curious, playful, keen-eyed, passionate writers – really do make excellent company. I hope you've found that in these pages too.

Will Harris, poet and essayist

I think the only thing that matters is whether your work is reward-ing – not whether it's good.

David Sedaris, essayist and performer

When I was young, perhaps because I came from a big family, I so desperately wanted attention. I tried being an artist, and I tried acting, and then I stumbled upon writing when I was twenty. I guess I broke the world into two groups at that point: there are people who pay someone to listen to their problems, and there are people who get paid to tell the world their problems. I really wanted to be in group number two.

The attention, and the fact that I earned it, means the world to me. Every night, when I walk to the podium at the theatre, it feels great. I remember the first time in college that I wrote something and the teacher asked me to read it in class: people laughed, and I thought, 'Nothing has ever felt this good.' I had put the words on paper, and I'd arranged them and I had rewritten it, and the work I'd put into it paid off. The sound of laughter, that's what does it for me. If you aren't writing humour, how do you know people are listening? I don't know what it takes to get up in front of people and read something serious for an hour, but I sure don't have it.

I sometimes notice that while something painful or embar-rassing is happening to me, I'm thinking about how I'm going to tell my friends later, and I'm looking forward to that. Do you find that it helps you through the painful moments of life – the knowledge that you can make it funny later?

A couple of years ago, a doctor stuck a wand up the hole in my penis and snaked it into my bladder. Once it was in my bladder, he started pumping in warm water. I couldn't pee and I didn't have any anaesthetic, and I was completely awake. I thought, 'I'm going to . . . write about . . . this . . . for the *New . . . Yorker*.' And I did.

If horrible things like that happened and I couldn't exploit them – if I just had to eat the plate of shit? I don't know how I would do it.

Raven Smith, columnist and essayist

The time it takes for a book to get from your head to being in front of other people – it's so long, that gamble. You throw the ball so high in the air, and it takes so long before you even know if you can catch it – it's just gone, for ages. I find that really hard, especially when you can write a tweet and know whether or not people like it in thirty seconds. But that's the thrill of it. Is this ball good enough to throw in the air and come back down in eighteen months? That's the fun of a book.

Emily St. John Mandel, novelist and screenwriter

What are the rewards for you of this arduous and long-winded process of writing novels?

It makes me happy. I love the feeling of building a world. I've always liked fixing things – I'll darn holes in my wool socks instead of buying new ones. There's something satisfying to me about taking something that has a problem and solving it, and that's really what revising a manuscript is.

Graham Norton, novelist

There's a lot of pleasure along the way. On a good day, when you're really connecting with the characters, there's nothing better than writing.

I used to interview writers and they'd say, '. . . and then the characters took on a life of their own', and I'd think, 'Shut up.' But of course, that does happen. You're typing away and you suddenly realise what's going to happen in a page and a half, and it's thrilling, because you just can't wait to get there. Those are the absolute best days.

Later in the process, I voice the audiobooks for my own novels. That's when you get a measure of the book, and recording them is embarrassing and horrific. You realise, 'Oh god, I really rushed that,' or 'This is going on a bit long, isn't it?' Everything is revealed, because it's too late to change it.

Again though, there are some wonderful parts. There's usually some big engineer there who couldn't care less. He's thinking, 'Is he *still* reading that book?' – and then suddenly, your own story moves you to tears. You can hear the engineer's eyes rolling on the other side of the glass. 'God, I thought it was bad before,' he's thinking, 'but now he's crying!'

Anna Hope, novelist

I think writing, on some level, feels subversive, because it's such a deep joy. The solitude is so incredibly rich and wonderful that it feels like, 'Am I allowed to have this much pleasure?' Then the validation that what you're doing is meeting readers, and living in their minds and hearts, is extraordinary. It means that I can carry on doing this thing, which continues to be a dream come true.

What are you proudest of when you look back over the years that you've spent writing?

Writing myself to equilibrium. I don't write for therapy, but my day-to-day life was definitely less happy before I was a writer. There's something about having this space and this practice, which is where I meet myself; it's been a really wonderful thing. I love seeing people like Judith Kerr, who just wrote to the end without retiring.

I'm also incredibly proud that I have helped to support my family through it. I remember reading an interview with Sebastian Barry. A journalist had come to his house, and Barry put his hand on the table and said, 'I paid for this with a novel.' I read it when I was working in a call centre, and I thought, 'I really want that.' To be able to say, 'Actually I paid for this table with my novel' – the thought of it makes me feel emotional, because I did my time waitressing and on the phones. It's amazing that you can take what we do – just sitting here, imagining things – and turn it into food, and tables.

Jon Ronson, storyteller and author

Throughout your career, you've chosen to research and write about experiences that many people would be intimidated by: spending time with extremists, or in a high-security psychiatric hospital . . . Where did your determination come from?

I remember that Louis Theroux was once asked a similar question, and his reply was 'Not doing it feels worse.' I think that's a good answer. A story not told, or an adventure not had, feels worse than doing something frightening and stressful and tiring. Also, I had a bad time growing up in Cardiff – I wasn't popular and I was bullied quite a lot, so maybe I felt a desperate need to succeed, to heal the wounds of my earlier years. Maybe I just wanted a solid place in the world. Then I realised that, for whatever reason, I knew how to do it. I just knew how to write.

I interviewed Randy Newman once and I asked him why he did it – why he spent his life writing songs. He said, 'It's how I judge myself and how I feel better.' Somewhere along the line, that happened to me. Writing became how I judged myself and how I felt better.

Georgia Pritchett, screenwriter

If I don't do some writing every single day, I feel sad – so I just make sure I do. It's the one thing I've never been confused about: I always knew, from before I could write, that I wanted to be a writer. I think my first 'book', in heavy quotation marks, was a biography of my hamster.

You write in your memoir My Mess Is a Bit of a Life *about being a child and sitting with your grandpa, V. S. Pritchett, while he was writing short stories. Was that formative?*

I think it really was. He lived in a pretty chaotic household, and there was something very calm and peaceful about watching him work. I saw then that it could be something that was not only incredibly creatively fulfilling, but also a lifeline or an oasis. Writing can be almost therapeutic – not just something you like doing, but something you kind of need to do.

Michael Rosen, poet and author

What is it about writing that makes it therapeutic?

I think there's a sense that you're getting it out of yourself – it's relief and release. Then there's a sense that you've made an order of it. Now, you've got to be a bit careful here: it's not *the* order, because you could express anything in thirty different ways, but it is an order. Your feelings can seem uncontrollable, like a formless miasma, swirling around. If you can then put them into a shape and a structure, that helps. It enables you to critique them. They're outside of yourself.

Then you can look at what you've written and ask yourself questions. Is that honest? Is that authentic? Is it how I am? You can make comparisons – to other bits of writing, to other people, and things that other people say. Later you can compare it to yourself in a month's time, two months' time, eight months' or two years' time. I can look at *Michael Rosen's Sad Book*, which I wrote after my son Eddie died, and say to myself, 'I don't feel like that now.' It captured me at a particular moment, and I feel glad about that.

The thing about comparisons is they're very cool. I don't mean cool in a groovy sense; I mean there's no heat in analogising. It's a bit forensic, and again, that's a relief. It cools down the heat in all that swirling, whirling watery stuff.

There's one other little piece, which is that you can be satisfied. If you're in difficulty – depressed, in agony, because of bereavement, or because somebody's deserted you – to do something that makes you satisfied . . . well, that's better than feeling depressed, isn't it? It's analogous to me writing about my family who were killed in the Holocaust. There's no relief from that, but there's a satisfaction in having found out about it, put it down on paper and shared it, and had people responding to it. There's a satisfaction in the midst of the tragedy.

Liane Moriarty, novelist

When I was a little girl, I just loved to write stories. I loved it in exactly the same way that I loved other things in my life, like riding a bike. When I'm sitting down to write now, I'm always searching for that uncomplicated pleasure that I used to get from writing when I was a little girl – with no self-consciousness at all.

My dad discovered that my sister and I liked to write, and he used to commission us to write stories for him; he gave us our first publishing deals. I remember how that made us feel very validated, to sit down as if this was our job. I have to say, it's never worn off, that feeling of, 'This is such a privilege – to sit at my desk and be paid to make up stories.' I can't believe that I get to do that.

Two of your novels, Big Little Lies *and* Nine Perfect Strangers, *have been adapted into major TV series. How has the success of those adaptations affected your career as a novelist?*

Well, it's obviously brought me many more readers who would otherwise never have heard of my books, so I'm very grateful for that. It's also meant some glamorous interludes, like going to the Emmys, and some fascinating insights into another world. I didn't expect to enjoy it as much as I did – the fun of seeing the whole process. I always describe it as just a really lovely perk of the job, and I've made some new friends, which again wasn't something I expected.

I feel I was very lucky, but it's still not the point of what I do, which is the novels. I never want to sit down to write a new book with the future adaptation in my mind. It's about the novel.

I feel very proud when readers tell me what my books have meant to them. Some people have said that my books got them through difficult times, with sick parents or children, because they're easy reads and have been a distraction or a comfort. In the signing lines at book events, sometimes I get quite teary – we all get teary. I've written about infertility, so women have come up and thanked me for that, and sometimes I've written the happy ending that they haven't had yet, because they're still on that journey. I wrote *Big Little Lies* about domestic violence, and a woman came up to me and said, 'I gave a copy of this book to all my friends and said, "This is me."' That was her way of letting her friends know what she'd been through. It's those reactions from readers that make it all worthwhile.

Sathnam Sanghera, journalist, novelist and non-fiction writer

To write about the issues I write about – social mobility, class, race, empire – is to stir up a hornets' nest. I get really angry about certain things, and I don't want to change that. I think it's important, I believe in things – but it also invites a lot of hostility. We're in the age of the culture war, and to be a writer nowadays sometimes involves being a soldier; you've got to fight, it's part of the job. I wouldn't complain about the criticism and the abuse and the occasional death threats. I think it means that I'm doing good work.

Elif Shafak, novelist

In countries like Turkey, a book is not a personal item. You don't put it back on your bookshelf when you finish reading it. You pass it on, you give it to your best friend, and the best friend shares it with her auntie, and the auntie sends it to her son who is doing his military service, and before you know it, a group of soldiers are reading the same book. I have seen a copy of one of my novels underlined by different coloured pens, because maybe five or six people have read the same copy. That word of mouth, that sharing, is incredibly heart-warming, and it matters a lot to me.

During the writing process though, novelists are solitary creatures. We don't know teamwork. Sometimes we have inflated egos. We think we're gods, you know – we create characters, we kill characters. You produce a lot on your own, so you need to have an inner garden. You really need to love what you're doing. Sometimes you will succeed, sometimes you will fail – you will fall down, get up and keep walking. What matters is, do you really love the art of storytelling?

Cressida Cowell, children's writer and illustrator

You wrote twelve books in the How to Train Your Dragon *series; you've sold over eleven million copies in thirty-eight languages, and it's been made into films and TV series by DreamWorks. What is it like to write a story that then takes flight – excuse the dragon pun – and has multiple lives after it has left you?*

It's been such a positive experience for me, because I love those films, and I was very close to the film-makers. I'm trying to write books that make you laugh and cry, and make you think about what it takes to be a hero and about looking after the environment, and the movies had all of those themes, even though they departed from the storyline of the books. All three films were Oscar-nominated. It's incredibly rare to have that experience and be that lucky.

It was also interesting, because I put a lot of my feelings about my father into *How to Train Your Dragon*. I was a parent by then, and I was thinking about how I was parented; having a film made out of something that is very personal to you, on such a huge scale, feels quite strange. You have to be very generous, I think. You either say, 'No, I'm not going to let this happen,' or you have to understand that you're giving it to somebody and trusting them to make something wonderful out of it.

You can't have control. With a book, you do have so much control: I'm the writer, I'm the illustrator, I'm acting it out in my writing shed, I'm doing the dialogue. A film just isn't that. It's a massive risk, because so many things have to come together. I have been very, very lucky that the end result was wonderful, because it would be heartbreaking otherwise – but the thing is, you always have the books, and the books are complete in themselves. I felt it was worth taking a risk, and I'm glad I did.

Meg Mason, novelist

Sorrow and Bliss has had a lot of attention. At one stage, the tabloids had pictures of the film-maker Olivia Wilde reading it on a yacht with her then boyfriend, the singer and actor Harry Styles. What has that kind of success been like for you?

That was just too funny. There was a huge discussion among their fans when the pictures emerged: 'What book is that?' There isn't really a part of the brain that can absorb all of that. There's not a part of your frontal lobe for when celebrities read your book; I just have to put it to one side. It's the same with it being made into a film: I can't imagine actors in it, or what that would all be like. I feel quite disconnected from it now that it's in the hands of the Olivia Wildes of this world.

It's funny – I think a positive response often lands a bit like that. If somebody criticises something I've done, then I take that quite seriously, but if they praise something, while it's lovely, I almost feel that it's got nothing to do with me. Maybe it's like that.

Absolutely, but I've also really tried hard not to let myself credit any of it to luck. I don't know if it's a particular thing that women struggle with, or whether it is more universal, but when something that we do succeeds, or we get to a certain level in our career, a lot of us are quick to say, 'Oh, I was just really lucky,' or 'It landed at the right time.' Actually, if you really look at it, luck doesn't come into it at all. If you were in the right place at the right time, it's only because you forced your way into being there.

I guess that's the part that I let myself feel rewarded for. Of course, there's luck involved with people picking it up and finding it, posting online about it and things like that – but the reason it exists is not because of luck. It's because I kept returning to the shed to work on it every single morning.

Jesse Armstrong, screenwriter

I love the feeling of 'I can't wait to show this to someone.' For me, the excitement is connected to a sense of transgression. 'I don't think anyone's quite done this before. Am I allowed to be this peculiar, or raw, or honest?'

Rumaan Alam, novelist

When you look at your writing life so far, what do you feel the most proud of?

You know, I'll tell you: it's the relationships I have with other writers who I consider truly great, and the notion that they would ever consider me at all engaged in the business that they are in.

I just got a copy of a book from a writer who is older than me, who I adore and have adored my entire career. It's very plausible that this writer's publisher has a publicity assistant who likes my book, and said, 'Hey, you know what? You should send a copy to Rumaan Alam.' Even if that's the reason, I don't care. Getting this book directly from this writer in their home, with a note saying, 'I wanted you to have this,' was so, so meaningful to me. I wish I could go back in time and tell the twenty-year-old who was reading this writer's work that someday he'd get a book from them as a gift. It blows my mind.

Grace Dent, restaurant critic, YA writer and memoirist

When I was at university, I wrote for fanzines. I wanted to do things where I could be opinionated and a bit bolshy, and I found that you can type out what you think of a certain clique, or a trend, or other people's pretension – and it doesn't have to be 6,000 words of incredibly good critical prose, you can literally do a list – and it will move people. It will make people think, 'Oh god, I love Grace Dent,' or even, 'I cannot stand her. How is she getting away with this?' I loved that.

At nineteen or twenty years old, I would write something for the student newspaper, and that feeling on publication day of walking through the campus, and people meeting your eye and going, 'Oh, I've just read the thing you wrote, and it's amazing!' – that's really addictive. We all want that feeling of being appreciated, or even just noticed; I was young, and it's as lovely as somebody being in love with you. But it's also completely double-edged, because nowadays, for every time I have a wave of love come at me for something I've written, there are thousands of people looking at it going, 'Why is she getting that?' They're just waiting for something to come along that's maybe not as good.

Wendy Erskine, short-story writer

Your first collection, Sweet Home, *was really well-reviewed. It was a book of the year in the* Guardian, *the* TLS *and various others, and it won the Butler Literary Award. That's a remarkable success – especially for a short-story collection, because they don't always get that much attention. What was that like for you?*

Well, I suppose the first thing was getting the kind of attention where you have to do interviews about your book. That was simultaneously quite nice and quite strange, because I realised how very, very carefully some people had read it, and that they'd picked up on things that I hadn't considered.

In some of those early interviews, I said very dopey things. There was one where I said something like, 'I'm trying to deal with the biggest themes known to mankind.' It just sounded so pompous and utterly ridiculous. I got a text immediately from a friend, saying, 'Thank goodness – after all these centuries, someone's finally got around to it.'

Getting longlisted and shortlisted for prizes was absolutely a delight. At the same time, I've read amazing stuff that has won no prizes whatsoever.

Having books published has made me feel quite proud of what I do in my day job, which is teaching English. I love being in the world of writing, and I've really enjoyed the people that I've met and the interesting stuff I've ended up doing – but it's very different to the world of working in a school, which is a collaborative thing. At school, I work with a group of people for the benefit of another group of people, and most of the time, it's fairly egoless – it's not really about the individual at all.

The world of books isn't so much that. It is much more about the individual. I enjoy that too – but it's not the whole thing about life.

Maggie O'Farrell, novelist

What do you get out of writing?

All I can say is that I always had the urge to do it. I don't really know why or where it came from – none of my family are writers – but even when I was five or six, I just wanted to put words down on paper. I used to spend all my pocket money on stationery, and I still do.

I've done lots of different jobs, and writing is the one that I find most satisfying intellectually, emotionally and mentally. It completely satisfies an urge in me to work something out. When I set off to write a book, I have many more questions than answers, and the act of writing the book is an attempt to answer them, although they don't all necessarily get answered.

There's a crossword-puzzle satisfaction to it, particularly as you get towards the end of a novel: you've got to make sure that the technical side of the book, the structure and grammar and plot, joins up with the emotional and psychological aspects. I love making them fit together as one entity, and I find great pleasure in making something appear that wasn't there before.

You've won the Women's Prize for Fiction, the Somerset Maugham Award, the National Book Critics Circle Award for Fiction, the Costa Novel Award . . . How do you feel about prizes?

Obviously it's a wonderful phone call to get, when somebody tells you that you've won something. It's always amazing when I get some kind of response from a reader, whether it's a prize jury, or somebody who writes to me and says, 'I read your book,' or even if it's just a child in a queue in a bookshop wanting to ask me about *Where Snow Angels Go*. For most of the life of a writer, it is you and your computer screen, or you and your blank page, and it's always incredible to have that connection, that moment, when you realise there are people out there who have read your book and, for whatever reason, want to tell you something.

But the thing about prizes is, I've been on enough juries to know that it is very, very arbitrary. A huge amount is to do with chance – there's somebody on the panel who happens to like your work. You just have to think of it as incredibly good luck, like winning the lottery, and then you have to forget about it and move on, because you've got to get back to the work.

Brandon Taylor, novelist

Your first novel was shortlisted for the Booker Prize. What was that experience like?

I'm a long-time watcher of literary prizes, and I love to specu-
late with all my friends and make predictions. When I found out I
was longlisted, I thought, 'Well, I know book prizes. I will be able
to handle this.' I was totally wrong.

A lot of people pay attention to this prize. Everyone has their
feelings about it and their baggage, and they are not shy about
projecting that onto you. They often see you as a symptom of
degradation. People feel very strongly about both the longlist and
the shortlist, as is their right.

Suddenly everybody wants to talk to you, and everybody has
an opinion about what you're saying. I found myself putting up
more of a shell than I normally would, as it became clear to me
that the outward-facing part of the writer's life takes up so much
more space than I thought. I used to be such a brat when writers
would announce their tour and they were only doing five events. I
would think, 'Why don't you come to my city?' But now I totally
understand why writers are so tired. It's a demanding schedule.
I don't want to make this sound like a problem – it's an immense
honour and I felt so lucky. But there were moments when I felt
really exhausted and thought I would never write again, because I
was going to be on the publicity tour for so long.

The one thing that's changed the most in my perception,
though, is that I used to think there was a secret strategy to literary
prizes. Now that I've been through that experience, I think there is
no secret agenda and no secret calculus. Literary prizes are judged
by people who love books and have their own particular tastes and
criteria, and they're just selecting books and encouraging people
to read them. I feel much less cynical about the whole thing now
that I've experienced it from the other side.

Hugo Rifkind, newspaper columnist

It's incredibly wanky to go on about awards, but it's a massive relief to win them. I've won enough not to have to think, 'Shit, should I really be doing this?'

Ayòbámi Adébáyò, novelist

Your debut novel Stay with Me *was enormously successful, and you were still in your twenties when it was published. What was that like? Did it give you confidence for the second novel, or did it get in the way of the second novel?*

It was stupefying, really, and sometimes it still is. It was long-listed for the Women's Prize for Fiction less than a week after it was published. I think the longlist was announced at midnight, and that night I'd done the first event in London to promote the book. I got back from that and I went to bed. I knew the longlist was coming out but I did not imagine that it would be on it.

I remember waking up around 6 a.m. and my phone kept buzzing. I went on Twitter before checking anything else, and I saw the notification 'The Women's Prize followed you'. I thought, 'What is going on?' I was just so grateful for it. It was a book that took me a really long time to finish and also took a while to get an editor or publisher who would believe in it.

In some ways, it gave me confidence. For one, I had the sense that there would be publishers interested in the second book – because with a debut, as a writer, you're really going into the unknown. It also meant, though, that I needed to get out of my own mind. There's a freedom that you have with a first book that I'm not sure you ever get back: the freedom of not having an awareness of how an audience might interact with your work. With *Stay with Me*, I was not self-conscious in the initial stages of working on it. With the second novel, I needed to get back into that space where I'm really writing for myself. I'm trying to get the internal logic of the novel and stay faithful to that, without thinking, 'Oh, somebody might think this is too this, or too that.' Those are thoughts that I need to address much later in the process in order to keep going.

What are you most proud of, looking at your writing life so far?

I'm always proud of finishing something, because there are so many moments in the process where I'm tempted to give up. When I've done a number of drafts and I feel, 'OK, now I can send this out' – I really do feel very satisfied with myself.

Holly Bourne, novelist

I write books for the young adult market, and teenagers are lovely. If they really like your work, they tell you that. They do incredible things like make fan art – they'll draw pictures of my characters in a scene and send it to me, and I'll cry because it's so amazing.

One of the happiest moments of my career was the response to my Spinster Club books, which are about starting a feminist campaign group in school. So many young people went off and started their own Spinster Clubs and Fem Socs. Whenever I go into schools to do talks, I come out feeling wonderful, because teenagers are just so vibrant. Writing adult fiction is fulfilling too – but adults don't tend to be as enthusiastic and positive, in the giddy, contagious way that only a teenage girl can.

André Aciman, novelist, memoirist and essayist

The emails about *Call Me By Your Name* still come every day. It's constant. There's a group of people called the Peaches:* they're readers who are huge fans, and they've become friends with one another across the globe – so you have Peaches in the Philippines, in Indonesia, in New York and Paris, and so on. They manifest themselves at every reading I've given. There are 25,000 of them and they've written a book about their take on the novel, and they're publishing another one.

Is that a strange feeling for you – that you've created something that's gone on to have this different life?

I can't let it affect me. I'm still the exact same person and I don't think about success. It's supposed to uplift me, but it doesn't. I observe it from across the street, as it were, and it's nice to know that it's there. I know it's going to go away, and so I just move on.

Zoe Williams, journalist

What are your first memories of being interested in writing?

I went on a school trip once to an area where historically there had been a huge disaster, and then we had to come back and write a report about it. There was a prize for the best report, and I did not win that prize – but they did give me a made-up prize for the funniest account of the death of ninety-eight people. I mean, they genuinely found it hilarious. I wasn't even trying to be funny, but

---

* Aciman's 2007 novel and the film adaptation by Luca Guadagnino include a key scene involving a peach.

I remember thinking, 'This is really, really pleasing, for everybody to be laughing.' It turns out that I do like the attention.

I would hate to win the lottery, because then everybody would know that I'm only working as a journalist for attention, because I wouldn't want to stop. I always worry, 'What would I do if I was widowed?' Obviously, I love my husband – I would hate it if he died – but my main worry is that I wouldn't want to take that week off my newspaper column, but it would look bad if I didn't.

Geoff Dyer, non-fiction writer and novelist

I feel very grateful that I've been able to lead this writing life. I've written more books than I ever thought I would, and that's made my life better for me, in every way. I've been invited to more parties, and I've been kept happier as a result of it. There hasn't been a single downside to it that I can think of.

John Lanchester, novelist and non-fiction writer

I love the flow state – that thing of being lost in it. Moment by moment, hour by hour, day by day, I like writing; I love that sense of disappearing into it. It's something that the late Clive James once said: happiness is a by-product of absorption. I don't think it makes sense to pursue happiness in life because it's too elusive, but you can pursue absorption – you can pursue the thing that just sucks you in when you're doing it.

What are you proudest of when you look back at your writing life so far?

I don't think about that, you know. I'm proud of my books. I'm very proud of them. I'm glad this is what I've done with my life, and I wouldn't do it differently – but at the same time, in a funny way, I didn't write them.

My first book – which in a sense is what made everything possible, because it did really well and allowed me to become a full-time writer – came out in 1996. The person who wrote that book isn't here any more; I'm very, very different. It's a trick of memory to make yourself into this completely coherent person and think that you understand everything about yourself, you knew what you were doing, you had your eyes wide open, you thought it all through; I think those are the stories we tell about ourselves, but a lot of the time they're not true. So I'm very proud of my books, and at the same time – right here, right now – I'm more interested in what's next.

Acknowledgements

I'm indebted to every writer who gave their time for this book and to every guest of the *In Writing* podcast. These conversations are among the greatest joys of my life.

I'm also deeply grateful to have friends with whom I can talk off-record about creativity. Over the last two decades those discussions have helped me to develop my ideas and interests as a writer, and to understand who I am. In particular, I want to thank Tor Freeman (a million times), Hywel Livingstone, Hannah Marriott, Josh Parish and Craig Taylor. For practical wisdom, thank you Mia Levitin and Sathnam Sanghera: each of you encouraged me to get an agent and generously made introductions. I needed those nudges.

Many more friends kept me going while I wrote this book, including Emma Baxter-Wright, Kelly Bowerbank, Rosie Clifton Van Vliet, Sutanya Dacres, Lynn Enright, Jennifer Fogerty, Andy Goll, Hannah Meltzer, Denis Ntais, Gemma Peterson, Selina Redmore, Andrew Robertson, Jion Sheibani, Sandeep Tavare, Nat Wade, Harriet Walker and Helen Warrell. Anna Ho, Karly Last, Claire Livingstone, Emily Sargent and Kate Walsh went beyond the call of duty in checking in on every bit of the publishing process and managing never to sound bored. I love you all.

Thank you Ken and Marjorie Stephinson for telling me as a little girl that I was a writer; my English teachers, especially the endlessly inspiring Wendy Erskine; David Stafford, for teaching me about plot, and all my creative-writing tutors and cohort at Birkbeck. Thank you to the countless editors who taught me to be a better journalist.

My agent, Imogen Pelham: I had a good feeling about you from the moment we met. I'm so grateful for your shrewd judgement and magnificent handling of the submission process, for your moral support and sense of humour, and for our shared intellectual interest in reality TV (I don't believe much in star signs, but I believe in Geminis). Thank you to Diana Beaumont, who, when Imogen's daughter Thea arrived early, swooped in to act as my agent for a while and brought kindness, steely industry knowledge and Italian pastries. Heartfelt thanks also to Mackenzie Brady Watson – I appreciate everything you've done for me, and I'm so glad we met.

Oliver Holms, you're a talent. I'm honoured to have had you take my photograph. Thea, you were my lucky charm, and I'll never forget it.

Thanks to Shaun Usher for his excellent *Letters of Note*, which pointed me in the direction of historic writers moaning, in a relatable way, about the process – and to Matt Trinetti and Parul Bavishi from the London Writers' Salon for encouraging and supporting writers everywhere.

Thank you to the team at Granta Books for what will probably remain the most enjoyable professional meeting of my life, in February 2023, and for the enormous collective effort that brought this book into the world and improved it along the way. In particular,

I'd like to thank Jack Alexander, Catrina Conway, Isabella Depiazzi, Lamorna Elmer, Bella Lacey, Christine Lo, Rosie Morgan, Kate Shearman, George Stamp and Alison Worthington. Wonderful Laura Barber: I'm so grateful for all the cheerleading and patience, and for your brilliant editing, which made this a much stronger book. Anna Morrison, your cover design is just gorgeous.

My sister Ellie – my best friend and *the* best friend – and my clever, funny, loving parents, Maggie and Andy: thanks aren't enough.* I love you to bits, forever.

Thank you and love to Margaret Sinclair. Since before I could walk, I've watched you show warmth and kindness to everybody you meet; I can't believe my luck in knowing you. Thank you Peter Crisell for huge practical support, and always being ready to put the kettle on and open the biscuits. To all my aunts, uncles and cousins on both sides, and to Milo, Nancy, Ben and the Moores: you're the family I'd choose. I'm so glad you're the one I've got.

Finally, to listeners of the *In Writing* podcast and readers of the newsletter: you changed my life. Thank you.

---

* So instead, I've prepared a dramatic reading of the book, which I will perform for the family over three evenings this Christmas. There will be a quiz at the end to find out who was paying attention. Keep those hearing aids on!

Index